CPCU 530 Course Guide

The Legal Environment of Insurance
3rd Edition

American Institute for Chartered Property Casualty Underwriters/Insurance Institute of America

720 Providence Road • Suite 100 • Malvern, PA 19355-3433

Third Edition • Second Printing • January 2010

ISBN 978-0-89463-393-5

Contents

Study Materials Available for CPCU 530

Karen Porter, *The Legal Environment of Insurance,* 1st ed., 2005, AICPCU/IIA.

CPCU 530 *Course Guide,* 3rd ed., 2009, AICPCU/IIA (includes access codes for SMART Online Practice Exams).

CPCU 530 SMART Study Aids—Review Notes and Flash Cards, 2nd ed.

Student Resources

Catalog A complete listing of our offerings can be found in *Succeed*, the Institutes' professional development catalog, including information about:

- Current programs and courses
- Current textbooks, course guides, and SMART Study Aids
- Program completion requirements
- Exam registration

To obtain a copy of the catalog, visit our Web site at www.aicpcu.org or contact Customer Service at (800) 644-2101.

How to Prepare for Institute Exams This free handbook is designed to help you by:

- Giving you ideas on how to use textbooks and course guides as effective learning tools
- Providing steps for answering exam questions effectively
- Recommending exam-day strategies

The handbook is printable from the Student Services Center on the Institutes' Web site at www.aicpcu.org, or available by calling Customer Service at (800) 644-2101.

Educational Counseling Services To ensure that you take courses matching both your needs and your skills, you can obtain free counseling from the Institutes by:

- E-mailing your questions to advising@cpcuiia.org
- Calling an Institutes' counselor directly at (610) 644-2100, ext. 7601
- Obtaining and completing a self-inventory form, available on our Web site at www.aicpcu.org or by contacting Customer Service at (800) 644-2101

Exam Registration Information As you proceed with your studies, be sure to arrange for your exam.

- Visit our Web site at www.aicpcu.org/forms to access and print the Registration Booklet, which contains information and forms needed to register for your exam.
- Plan to register with the Institutes well in advance of your exam.

How to Contact the Institutes For more information on any of these publications and services:

- Visit our Web site at www.aicpcu.org
- Call us at (800) 644-2101 or (610) 644-2100 outside the U.S.
- E-mail us at customerservice@cpcuiia.org
- Fax us at (610) 640-9576
- Write to us at AICPCU/IIA, Customer Service, 720 Providence Road, Suite 100, Malvern, PA 19355-3433

Using This Course Guide

This course guide will help you learn the course content and prepare for the exam.

Each assignment in this course guide typically includes the following components:

Educational Objectives These are the most important study tools in the course guide. Because all of the questions on the exam are based on the Educational Objectives, the best way to study for the exam is to focus on these objectives.

Each Educational Objective typically begins with one of the following action words, which indicate the level of understanding required for the exam:

Analyze—Determine the nature and the relationship of the parts.

Apply—Put to use for a practical purpose.

Associate—Bring together into relationship.

Calculate—Determine numeric values by mathematical process.

Classify—Arrange or organize according to class or category.

Compare—Show similarities and differences.

Contrast—Show only differences.

Define—Give a clear, concise meaning.

Describe—Represent or give an account.

Determine—Settle or decide.

Evaluate—Determine the value or merit.

Explain—Relate the importance or application.

Identify or list—Name or make a list.

Illustrate—Give an example.

Justify—Show to be right or reasonable.

Paraphrase—Restate in your own words.

Summarize—Concisely state the main points.

Required Reading The items listed in this section indicate the study materials (the textbook chapter(s), course guide readings, or other assigned materials) that correspond to the assignment.

Outline The outline lists the topics in the assignment. Read the outline before the required reading to become familiar with the assignment content and the relationships of topics.

Key Words and Phrases These words and phrases are fundamental to understanding the assignment and have a common meaning for those working in insurance. After completing the required reading, test your understanding of the assignment's Key Words and Phrases by writing their definitions.

Review Questions The review questions test your understanding of what you have read. Review the Educational Objectives and required reading, then answer the questions to the best of your ability. When you are finished, check the answers at the end of the assignment to evaluate your comprehension.

Application Questions These questions continue to test your knowledge of the required reading by applying what you've studied to "hypothetical" real-life situations. Again, check the suggested answers at the end of the assignment to review your progress.

Sample Exam Your course guide includes either a sample exam (located at the back) or a code for accessing SMART Online Practice Exams (which appears on the inside back cover). Use this supplemental exam material to become familiar with the test format and to practice answering exam questions.

For courses that offer SMART Online Practice Exams, you can both download and print a sample credentialing exam and take full practice exams using the same software you will use when you take your credentialing exam. SMART Online Practice Exams are as close as you can get to experiencing an actual exam before taking one.

More Study Aids

The Institutes also produce supplemental study tools, called SMART Study Aids, for many of our courses. When SMART Study Aids are available for a course, they are listed on both page iii of this course guide and on the first page of each assignment. SMART Study Aids include Review Notes and Flash Cards and are excellent tools to help you learn and retain the information in each assignment.

CPCU Advisory Committee

F. Scott Addis, CPCU
The Addis Group

Chris Amrhein, AAI
Amrhein and Associates, Inc.

Scott A. Behrent, CPCU, AIC
Farm Family Casualty Insurance Company

Mark J. Browne, PhD
University of Wisconsin, Madison School of Business

Anne Crabbs, CPCU
State Auto Insurance Companies

Richard A. Derrig
OPAL Consulting

Eric A. Fitzgerald
Marshall, Dennehey, Warner, Coleman & Goggin

Joseph A. Gerber, Esq.
Cozen O'Connor

Dennis M. Halligan, CPCU
Farmers Group

Joseph S. Harrington, CPCU, ARP
American Association of Insurance Services

Frederick P. Hessenthaler, CPCU
Chubb & Son

Steven M. Horner, CPCU, CLU, AIM, ARM
Horner & Associates, LLC

Robert E. Hoyt, PhD, CLU, ChFC
University of Georgia

James Jones, CPCU, AIC, ARM, AIS
Katie School of Insurance & Financial Services

John J. Kelly, CPCU, CLU, ChFC, ARM
CPCU Society

Johannah Lipscher, CPCU, AIS
Zurich North America

Stanley L. Lipshutz, Esq., CPCU
Lipshultz & Hone Chartered & Interrisk Ltd.

Dennis F. Mahoney, CEBS, CFP
The Wharton School, University of Pennsylvania

Gregory Massey, CPCU, CIC, CRM, ARM
Selective Insurance Company of America

Michael McVey, CPCU, ARe
Penn National Insurance

Ronald M. Metcho, CPCU, ARM, AAI
Saul-Metcho Insurance

Robin K. Olson, CPCU
International Risk Management Institute, Inc.

Jesus Pedre, CPCU, AIC, AIS
Texas Department of Insurance

Brian P. Savko, CPCU
State Farm Insurance Companies

Wade E. Sheeler, CPCU
Grinnell Mutual Group

James A. Sherlock, CPCU, CLU, ARM
ACE, USA

Angela K. Sparks, CPCU
State Farm Insurance Companies

Christine A. Sullivan, CPCU, AIM
Allstate Insurance Company

Lawton Swan, CPCU, CLU, ARM, CSP, CMC
Interisk Corporation

Sean S. Sweeney, CPCU, RPLU, ARe
Phildelphia Insurance Company

Kenneth J. Swymer, Sr., EdD, CPCU
Liberty Mutual Group

Angela Viane, CPCU, AIS
Zurich North America

Andrew Zagrzejewski, CPCU, AIC
Farmers Group—Los Angeles Service Center

Direct Your Learning

Introduction to U.S. Law and Insurance Regulation

Educational Objectives

After learning the content of this assignment, you should be able to:

1. Describe the U.S. civil-law and common-law systems and classifications.

2. Describe the role of each of the following sources of U.S. law:

   a. Constitutions

   b. Legislative bodies

   c. Courts

   d. Executive branches

   e. Administrative agencies

3. Given a case, explain how each of the following U.S. Constitutional provisions applies:

   a. Congressional powers

   b. Commerce Clause

   c. Due Process Clause

   d. Equal Protection Clause

4. Given a case, explain how conflicts of law principles apply.

5. Given a case, apply court procedural and evidentiary rules.

6. Describe the forms of alternative dispute resolution (ADR).

7. Summarize administrative agency functions and powers and the judicial review of agency activities.

8. Describe the Privacy Act and Freedom of Information Act (FOIA) provisions.

9. Describe the roles of federal and state law in insurance regulation, and explain how those roles would apply in a case.

Study Materials

Required Reading:
▶ The Legal Environment of Insurance
  • Chapter 1

Study Aids:
▶ SMART Online Practice Exams
▶ SMART Study Aids
  • Review Notes and Flash Cards— Assignment 1

Outline

▶ **The U.S. Legal System**

  A. Civil-Law System

  B. Common-Law System

    1. Judicial Influence on Common Law

    2. The Evolution of Common Law

    3. Equity

  C. Classifications of U.S. Law

    1. Classification as Criminal or Civil Law

    2. Classification by Subject Matter

    3. Classification as Substantive or Procedural Law

▶ **Sources of U.S. Law**

  A. Constitutions

  B. Legislative Bodies

  C. Courts

    1. Federal Court System

    2. State Court Systems

    3. Conflicts of Law

  D. Executive Branches

    1. Administrative Agencies

▶ **Legal Procedures**

  A. Court Procedure

    1. Pretrial Procedure

    2. Trial Procedure

    3. Appeals

  B. Alternative Dispute Resolution

    1. Arbitration

    2. Mediation

    3. Negotiation

  C. Administrative Agency Procedure

    1. Agencies' Rulemaking Function

    2. Agencies' Adjudicatory Function

    3. Agencies' Investigative Powers

    4. Judicial Review

    5. Privacy and Freedom of Information Acts

▶ **Insurance Regulation**

  A. Federal Regulation

  B. State Insurance Regulation

  C. National Association of Insurance Commissioners (NAIC)

  D. Regulation of Insurers

  E. Insurance Producer Regulation

    1. Licensing and License Renewal

    2. Managing General Agents (MGAs)

    3. Surplus Lines Brokers

▶ **Summary**

▶ **Appendix—Constitution of the United States**

Don't spend time on material you have already mastered. The SMART Review Notes are organized by the Educational Objectives found in each course guide assignment to help you track your study.

Key Words and Phrases

Define or describe each of the words and phrases listed below.

Civil-law system (p. 1.3)

Doctrine of *stare decisis* (p. 1.4)

Equity (p. 1.6)

Criminal law (p. 1.7)

Civil law (p. 1.7)

Substantive law (p. 1.8)

Procedural law (p. 1.8)

Jurisdiction (p. 1.9)

Commerce Clause (p. 1.11)

Due Process Clause (p. 1.12)

Equal Protection Clause (p. 1.12)

Guest statute (p. 1.12)

National Association of Insurance Commissioners (NAIC) (p. 1.13)

Original jurisdiction (p. 1.13)

Appellate jurisdiction (p. 1.13)

General jurisdiction (p. 1.13)

Diversity jurisdiction (p. 1.14)

Appellate court (p. 1.15)

Writ of *certiorari* (p. 1.15)

Conflicts of law (p. 1.16)

Forum state (p. 1.17)

Administrative law (p. 1.18)

Allegation (p. 1.19)

Complaint (p. 1.19)

Plaintiff (p. 1.19)

Defendant (p. 1.19)

Pleading (p. 1.19)

Cause of action (p. 1.19)

Answer (p. 1.19)

Counterclaim (p. 1.19)

Motion (p. 1.19)

Motion to dismiss (p. 1.19)

Motion for judgment on the pleadings,
or motion for summary judgment (p. 1.20)

Discovery (p. 1.21)

Deposition (p. 1.21)

Interrogatories (p. 1.21)

Motion to produce (p. 1.21)

Direct examination (p. 1.23)

Cross-examination (p. 1.23)

Relevance (p. 1.23)

Materiality (p. 1.23)

Competence (p. 1.23)

Hearsay rule (p. 1.23)

General verdict (p. 1.24)

Special verdict (p. 1.24)

Res judicata (p. 1.24)

Collateral estoppel (p. 1.25)

Appeal (p. 1.25)

Appellant (p. 1.25)

Appellee (p. 1.25)

Alternative dispute resolution (ADR) (p. 1.26)

Arbitration (p. 1.26)

Mediation (p. 1.27)

Legislative rule (p. 1.28)

Interpretative rule (p. 1.28)

Procedural rule (p. 1.28)

Subpoena (p. 1.31)

Standing to sue (p. 1.32)

Final order (p. 1.32)

Exhaustion of administrative remedies (p. 1.32)

Zone examination (p. 1.39)

Managing general agent (MGA) (p. 1.40)

Review Questions

1. Describe the civil-law and common-law systems. (pp. 1.3–1.4)

2. Explain how the common law changes. (p. 1.4)

3. Distinguish between civil and criminal law. (p. 1.7)

4. Describe the respective roles of state constitutions and the federal Constitution. (pp. 1.9–1.10)

5. Explain how the U.S. Constitution grants congressional powers. (p. 1.11)

6. Explain why or why not state governments are required to provide due process. (p. 1.12)

7. Describe the purpose of uniform laws. (p. 1.13)

8. Give one example of a legal matter over which federal courts have original jurisdiction. (p. 1.14)

9. What are courts of general jurisdiction? (p. 1.13)

10. How can parties to a contract avoid conflicts of law? (p. 1.17)

11. Explain how the executive branches influence legislation.
    (pp. 1.17–1.18)

12. Describe the types and order of pleadings in pretrial procedure.
    (pp. 1.19–1.21)

13. Identify three bases for excluding evidence at trial. (p. 1.23)

14. Discuss whether appellate courts conduct new trials. (p. 1.26)

15. When is alternative dispute resolution (ADR) binding on the parties? (p. 1.26)

16. List the three types of administrative agency rules. (p. 1.28)

17. What actions can an administrative agency take after it has reviewed all comments about a proposed rule? (p. 1.29)

18. What must an appropriate notice, essential to due process, include in an administrative agency context? (p. 1.29)

▶▶

19. Describe the U.S. Constitutional limitations on agency investigations. (p. 1.31)

20. What is required before courts will review administrative agency decisions? (p. 1.32)

21. Briefly summarize the McCarran-Ferguson Act. (pp. 1.34–1.35)

22. What do NAIC model laws try to accomplish? (p. 1.37)

23. What must an applicant do to qualify for an insurance producer's license? (p. 1.40)

24. Explain why MGAs are subject to regulatory attention. (p. 1.41)

25. What must a producer do to qualify for a surplus lines broker license under the NAIC model act? (p. 1.41)

Application Questions

1. In 1852 the Midvale Township court wrote an opinion stating that, if a dog bites a person, the dog's owner must pay for the damages resulting from the dog bite, whatever the circumstances. In 1875 Midvale Township passed a law saying that any owner of a dog who allows that dog to run free is responsible for any damage the dog causes. In 1952 the local court wrote an opinion saying that dogs owned by green-eyed people could have "one free bite" unless the dog has shown vicious propensities. That is, if a dog bites a person for the first time, its green-eyed owner is not liable unless the dog previously had shown vicious propensities. However, upon the second bite, the dog owner with green eyes is liable.

   Mary, who has brown eyes, lives in Midvale. Her large dog, Sam, which had never shown any vicious propensities but had knocked a few people down, just bit Mary's neighbor. The neighbor is suing Mary.

   a. Describe how the common law applies here.

   b. What constitutional issue might apply to this case?

2. Peter is a resident of State Y, and Don is a resident of State Z. While Peter is driving in State Z, his car is struck by a car driven by Don. Peter is injured, and he files a lawsuit seeking $4,000 in property damage and $150,000 for personal injuries. Common law applies in both cases.

   a.   May Peter sue Don in the courts of State Z? Justify your answer.

   b.   May Peter sue Don in the federal courts? If not, why not?

   c.   Assuming, for this question, that Peter may sue Don in the federal courts, what is the source of the substantive law the federal courts will apply? Explain.

   d.   Again assuming that Peter may sue Don in the federal courts, what is the source of the procedural law the federal courts will follow? Explain.

3. Joyce slipped and fell on the icy parking lot in a shopping mall. She has consulted you as her lawyer about suing the mall owner for negligence. Advise her about what to expect in pretrial proceedings.

   a.   Describe the pleadings she must file.

   b.   Describe the tools that attorneys for Joyce and the mall owner may use to conduct discovery in this case.

4. Jack's truck was stopped at a stop sign. He did not see Mike's small car stopped behind him. Jack backed the truck up, crushed the front of Mike's car, and injured Mike, who ultimately sued Jack. At trial Mike's lawyer wishes to introduce the following evidence. Evaluate each of the following pieces of evidence as to its admissibility:

   a.   Jack's past record of parking tickets

   b.   Jack's past record of drug abuse

c. Wilma's testimony that she overheard Jack's first words to Mike at the accident scene: "Where'd you come from?"

5. Jane purchased a product that injured her. She is attempting to obtain money for her injury from the manufacturer of the product. Describe how each form of alternative dispute resolution (ADR) in the book could be a helpful way to resolve her dispute.

6. The Board of Health, an administrative agency with rule-making authority, adopted, without a formal hearing, a rule prohibiting tattooing by any unlicensed person. The rule, which was made final, was based on the opinion of medical experts on the Board of Health staff asserting a definite connection between tattooing and hepatitis. Several unlicensed persons who had been operating tattoo parlors sued to have the rule declared invalid.

a. Explain whether the unlicensed tattoo-parlor operators must seek further administrative action before appealing to the courts.

b. Explain whether the unlicensed tattoo-parlor operators have standing to sue and a right to appeal.

c. Did the adoption of the rule affect the unlicensed tattoo-parlor operators' constitutional rights in any way? Explain.

d. The unlicensed tattoo-parlor operators argue that the rule was arbitrary and capricious in depriving them of their right to engage in a business. Explain the merits, if any, of such an argument.

Answers to Assignment 1

NOTE: These answers are provided to give students a basic understanding of acceptable types of responses. They often are not the only valid answers and are not intended to provide an exhaustive response to the questions.

Review Questions

1. A civil-law system has a comprehensive code of written laws or statutes. A common-law system is a body of law derived from court decisions as opposed to statutes or constitutions.

2. Common law changes through court examination of precedent. A court may apply a precedent to new cases or discard it if it has lost its usefulness, or may make landmark decisions that depart from precedent.

3. Criminal law applies to acts society deems so harmful to the public welfare that government is responsible for prosecuting and punishing the perpetrators. Civil law applies to legal matters that are not governed by criminal law, protecting rights and providing remedies for breaches of duties owed to others.

4. The U.S. (federal) Constitution is the "supreme Law of the Land." Each state has its own constitution, which is the supreme law of that state, subservient only to the U.S. Constitution. The U.S. Constitution always prevails over a state constitution in case of a conflict.

5. The Constitution establishes the express powers of Congress and the implied powers to pass laws necessary to implement the express powers.

6. States are required to provide due process because the U.S. Constitution's Fourteenth Amendment extends Fifth Amendment Due Process protection to state government actions.

7. Uniform laws minimize confusion and conflict resulting from variations in state and local laws.

8. An example of a legal matter over which federal courts have original jurisdiction would be an admiralty or maritime case.

9. Courts of general jurisdiction are courts that hear a variety of types of cases.

10. Parties to a contract can avoid conflicts of law by including in the contract an agreement about which state's laws will apply if a dispute arises.

11. An executive branch can recommend, approve, or veto laws. The executive can appoint heads of administrative agencies to assist in enforcing laws and can influence agencies' rules and regulations.

12. The plaintiff files a complaint setting out allegations, stating a cause of action, and requesting a remedy. The court issues a summons notifying the defendant of the lawsuit that includes a copy of the complaint and that sets out a timeframe for the defendant to answer. The defendant files an answer stating why the plaintiff should not win the case. The answer may include counterclaims. Alternatively, the defendant may file an entry of appearance. After receiving the defendant's answer, the plaintiff files a reply.

13. Three bases for excluding evidence at trial are that the evidence lacks relevance, materiality, or competence.

14. Appellate courts do not conduct new trials but decide whether the lower court has applied the law appropriately to a case.

15. ADR can be binding on parties when they have agreed in advance that it will be binding.

16. The three types of administrative agency rules including the following:
    (1) Legislative rules
    (2) Interpretative rules
    (3) Procedural rules

17. After reviewing comments about a proposed rule, an agency can do one of the following:
    - Adopt the originally proposed rule
    - Make minimal or extensive changes to the rule
    - Nullify the proposed rule

18. An appropriate notice, for due process, would include the following:
    - A statement of the hearing time, place, and nature
    - A statement of the hearing's legal authority and jurisdiction
    - Reference to the statute or rule involved
    - A short, clear statement of the matters at issue

19. The U.S. Constitution places the following limitations on agency investigations:
    - Fourth Amendment protection against unreasonable searches and seizures
    - Fifth Amendment protection against self-incrimination

20. To take an administrative action to a court for judicial review, the following must have occurred:
    - The plaintiff must have standing to sue.
    - The agency must have issued a final order in the case.
    - The plaintiff must have exhausted all administrative remedies.

21. The McCarran-Ferguson Act permits each state to regulate the business of insurance conducted within its borders.

22. NAIC model laws attempt to promote uniform insurance regulation among the states.

23. An applicant must fulfill the following requirements to qualify for an insurance producer's license:
    - Be of at least minimum age
    - Have an appointment from a licensed insurance company
    - Have completed the requisite application forms
    - Have satisfactorily completed the examination requirement

24. Regulatory attention to MGAs evidences increasing concern about the role that some MGAS have played in major insurer insolvencies.

25. A producer must pass a DOI-approved exam and post a bond of a specified amount to become a surplus lines broker under the NAIC model act.

Application Questions

1. a. The original court case in 1852 was the law in Midvale Township and provided that a dog owner must pay damages for any bite. The 1875 statutory law added to the case law by providing that, in addition to damages for bites, a dog owner must pay for any damage caused by a dog running free. The 1952 court case eliminated damages for first bites of dogs owned by green-eyed people only. In summary, each of these laws supplemented the others and did not overrule them. The township also could have legally passed statutory law changing case law.

   b. This law is a violation of the constitutional right to equal protection of the laws (Fourteenth Amendment) in that it discriminates unfairly and arbitrarily against people who do not have green eyes.

2. a. State Z is the state where Don lives and the state where the accident occurred, so there is no reason Peter cannot sue Don in State Z.

   b. Peter and Don are citizens of two different states, and the amount in controversy of $154,000 probably meets the minimum amount necessary for federal jurisdiction. Therefore, diversity jurisdiction applies, and Peter can file suit in federal court.

   c. The federal court may apply the substantive law of the state in which the court is located. Therefore, if Peter sues in the federal court in State Y, that state's substantive law will apply. Alternatively, if Peter sues in the federal court in State Z, that state's substantive law will apply.

   d. The federal court will apply its own procedural rules.

3. a. Joyce must file a complaint to commence suit. If the defendant files an answer, Joyce may file a reply to that answer.

   b. The discovery process will involve acquisition of evidence by both parties using the following tools:

   - Depositions—Each party may depose each witness. For example, Joyce's lawyer may ask oral questions of the person who was supposed to keep the parking lot safe. Depositions are transcribed to preserve a written record.

   - Interrogatories—Each party also may file written questions called interrogatories. For example, Joyce's lawyer may send interrogatories to the mall management, and management must provide written answers to the interrogatories.

   - Motions to produce—Each party also may request the court to order the other party to provide documents via motions to produce. For example, Joyce's lawyer may request written documents recording any other safety measures taken by the mall relating to the parking lot before the accident.

4. a. Jack's past record of parking tickets is probably irrelevant and immaterial to this case and would therefore be inadmissible.

   b. Jack's past record of drug abuse could be relevant and material, and therefore admissible, if it is connected in some way to this case, such as by allegation of Jack's drug abuse at the time of the accident or at the time of other accidents.

   c. Jack's first words to Mike are relevant and material and therefore admissible to show that he did not, for whatever reason, see Mike. A hearsay objection might be raised, but one of the many exceptions to the hearsay rule may apply.

5. Any form of ADR could help speed up the process for Jane. Litigation is lengthy and expensive, and Jane probably needs more immediate relief. With arbitration, the parties would agree in advance to abide by the arbitrator's decision. Mediation can help Jane and the manufacturer analyze their dispute and devise a compromise. Negotiation can provide Jane with a direct route to settlement of her claim. A mini-trial or summary jury trial could aid Jane in negotiating a settlement by showing what evidence and arguments would be presented in a trial and what a jury might decide in the case.

6. a. The complainants first should exhaust all administrative remedies. No court will hear the case without the complainants' first having challenged the rule before the Board of Health, under administrative procedures.

    b. Because the new rule applies directly to and adversely affects unlicensed persons who operate tattoo parlors, and because these complainants are unlicensed persons who operate tattoo parlors, they have standing to sue.

    c. The tattoo-parlor operators can allege that their property (earnings, shops) was taken away without due process of law. They also might allege an equal protection clause violation. It is not clear who can tattoo, with the law saying only that lay persons cannot tattoo. There must be some rational basis for this law, such as that lay persons are more likely, in some way, to spread hepatitis.

    d. This argument is similar to the constitutional argument in that the facts, as given, do not establish the rationale for excluding lay persons from the right to tattoo. If the Board of Health can show why these lay persons should be excluded from the tattoo business, then there may be no arbitrary and capricious argument.

Direct Your Learning

Contracts: Formation; Agreement and Capacity to Contract

Educational Objectives

After learning the content of this assignment, you should be able to:

1. Identify the elements of a legally enforceable contract.

2. Classify a contract presented in a case under one or more of the following types:

   a. Bilateral and unilateral contracts

   b. Executed and executory contracts

   c. Express and implied contract

   d. Void contracts and voidable contracts

3. Apply the requirements of the following in a case:

   a. An offer

   b. An acceptance

4. Describe the contractual capacity of the following and apply the legal principles concerning their capacity in a case:

   a. Minors

   b. Insane people

   c. Intoxicated people

   d. Corporations

5. Describe the contractual capacity of the following:

   a. Insurers

   b. Insurance producers

   c. Insureds

Study Materials

Required Reading:

▶ The Legal Environment of Insurance
  • Chapter 2

Study Aids:

▶ SMART Online Practice Exams

▶ SMART Study Aids
  • Review Notes and Flash Cards— Assignment 2

Outline

▶ **Contract Formation**

▶ **Types of Contracts**

   A. Bilateral and Unilateral Contracts

   B. Executed and Executory Contracts

   C. Express and Implied Contracts

   D. Voidable Contracts and Void Contracts

▶ **First Element of an Enforceable Contract: Agreement**

   A. Offer

      1. Intent to Contract

      2. Definite Terms

      3. Communication to Offeree

      4. Duration and Termination

   B. Acceptance

      1. Acceptance by Offeree

      2. Unconditional and Unequivocal Acceptance

      3. Offeree's Communication of Acceptance

▶ **Second Element of an Enforceable Contract: Capacity to Contract**

   A. Minors' Contracts

   B. Insane Persons' Contracts

   C. Intoxicated Persons' Contracts

   D. Artificial Entities' Contracts

   E. Insurance Contracts

      1. Insurer's Capacity

      2. Insurance Producer's Capacity

      3. Insured's Capacity

▶ **Summary**

Reduce the number of Key Words and Phrases that you must review. SMART Flash Cards contain the Key Words and Phrases and their definitions, allowing you to set aside those cards that you have mastered.

Key Words and Phrases

Define or describe each of the words and phrases listed below.

Contract (p. 2.4)

Promisor (p. 2.4)

Promisee (p. 2.4)

Third-party beneficiary (p. 2.4)

Breach of contract (p. 2.4)

Privity of contract (p. 2.4)

Agreement (p. 2.4)

Capacity to contract (p. 2.4)

Consideration (p. 2.5)

Bilateral contract (p. 2.5)

Unilateral contract (p. 2.5)

Executed contract (p. 2.5)

Executory contract (p. 2.6)

Express contract (p. 2.6)

Implied-in-fact contract (p. 2.6)

Implied-in-law contract (p. 2.6)

Voidable contract (p. 2.7)

Void contract (p. 2.7)

Offer (p. 2.8)

Counteroffer (p. 2.12)

Option contract (p. 2.13)

Acceptance (p. 2.13)

Forbearance (p. 2.17)

Substantial performance (p. 2.17)

Competent party (p. 2.19)

Restitution (p. 2.20)

Review Questions

1. List the elements of a contract. (p. 2.3)

2. Can a party that is not in privity of contract ever sue for breach of the contract? (p. 2.4)

3. Are implied contracts actual agreements between the parties? Explain. (p. 2.6)

4. List the elements of an offer. (p. 2.8)

5. Are advertisements offers? Explain. (p. 2.9)

6. How does a court determine reasonable certainty to determine whether an offer exists? (p. 2.10)

▶▶

7. List five factors regarding duration and termination that are key to determining whether an offer is binding. (pp. 2.11–2.12)

8. List the elements of acceptance. (p. 2.14)

9. Can silence ever be acceptance? (p. 2.16)

10. Identify parties that might be incompetent to contract. (p. 2.19)

11. What are minors' rights and duties under their contracts? (pp. 2.20–2.21)

12. What are the rights and duties of parents under minors' contracts? (p. 2.22)

13. What are insane persons' rights and duties under contracts? (pp. 2.22–2.23)

14. Under what circumstances will intoxication allow a party to avoid a contract? (p. 2.24)

15. Can an insurer avoid a contract entered into in a state in which the insurer is unlicensed? (pp. 2.25–2.26)

▶▶

Application Questions

1. Alex was a young high school student whose parents died in an automobile accident. He was left penniless and without means of support. A local merchant invited Alex to live with him and his family, with room, board, clothing, and all other necessities provided. Alex worked around the house and also worked after school in the merchant's store. Two years later, after Alex's graduation from high school, the merchant died, and his family told Alex to move out. Alex then entered a claim against the merchant's estate for the reasonable value of services rendered. Analyze the possibilities of his recovering the reasonable value of services under the following theories:

   a. Express contract

   b. Implied-in-fact contract

   c. Implied-in-law contract

2. On January 13, Daniel signed a contract to purchase certain real estate owned by Patricia and mailed it to her for her signature, with a note asking Patricia to mail the contract back. Patricia received the contract on January 15, immediately signed it, and put the contract addressed to Daniel in the mail. Later the same day, Patricia phoned Daniel and repudiated the contract. Daniel received the contract on January 17. Is there a valid and binding contract? Explain why or why not.

3. Oliver owned a car and wanted to sell it privately rather than trade it in on a new car. Oliver's neighbor Tom expressed interest in the car, and Oliver offered it to Tom for $1,000, saying, "Think it over, and call me tonight." Tom did not call that night. The next day, a colleague of Oliver's at the office learned of the car, and before Oliver could set a price, she offered him $1,500 for it. Oliver said, "You've got a deal!" When Oliver went home that night, Tom came over and said, "I'll take it." Oliver then told Tom, regretfully, that he had already sold the car to a colleague at work. Is Oliver legally bound to Tom? Why or why not?

4. Sue is under the age of majority. She purchased a used automobile from Fred for $1,200, paying $300 down and contracting to pay the remaining $900 in monthly installments plus interest at the rate of 20 percent. Sue appeared to be an adult, and when Fred inquired concerning Sue's age, she assured him that she was of age. Two weeks after Sue actually became of legal age, the car was totally demolished while lawfully parked. Sue claims the right to disaffirm the contract for the automobile and get back all the money she paid on the basis that she did not have capacity to contract because of her minority. Fred maintains that Sue's parents are liable for the remainder of the debt and that he is entitled to the full purchase price from Sue because the automobile was a necessity for Sue to go to and from her place of employment. Evaluate each of these contentions fully.

Answers to Assignment 2 Questions

NOTE: These answers are provided to give students a basic understanding of acceptable types of responses. They often are not the only valid answers and are not intended to provide an exhaustive response to the questions.

Review Questions

1. The following are the elements of a contract:
    - Agreement
    - Capacity to contract
    - Consideration
    - Legal purpose

2. Ordinarily, a party cannot sue for breach of contract without being in privity of contract (unless that person is a third-party beneficiary of the contract).

3. Yes, implied contracts are agreements that are intended by parties, either by assumption or tacitly, even though the parties might not have expressed their agreements explicitly.

4. The following are the elements of an offer:
    - Intent to contract
    - Definite terms
    - Communication to offeree

5. Advertisements are not offers; they are invitations to negotiate or to make offers, expressing no present intent to contract.

6. To determine reasonable certainty, a court may ask whether an offer's terms are clear enough to provide a basis for a remedy if default occurs.

7. The following five factors regarding duration and termination are key to determining whether an offer is binding:
    (1) Lapse of time
    (2) Operation of law
    (3) Offeree's rejection
    (4) Counteroffers
    (5) Offeror's revocation

8. The following are the elements of acceptance:
    - The acceptance must be made by the offeree.
    - The acceptance must be unconditional and unequivocal.
    - The offeree must communicate the acceptance to the offeror by appropriate word or act.

9. No, an offeree's silence cannot be acceptance.

10. Parties that might be incompetent to contract include the following:
    - Minors
    - Insane persons
    - Intoxicated persons
    - Artificial entities

11. The law protects minors from disposing of their property while they are underage. Generally, a minor can assert minority as a defense against liability in contracts, except those involving the purchase of necessaries.

12. Parents are generally not liable for minor children's contracts unless a parent cosigns, the child has acted on the parent's behalf or at the parent's direction, or a parent has neglected or refused to pay for necessaries for the minor.

13. Any agreement entered by a person adjudged by a court to be insane is void, except for a contract for necessaries. A contract by a person who claims to be insane, but has not been judged so by a court, is voidable under certain conditions.

14. An intoxicated person can avoid a contract if the person did not know a contract was forming or did not understand the legal consequences of acts purporting to form the contract.

15. Policies sold by insurers not licensed to do business in a state are enforceable against them.

Application Questions

1. a. Nothing in this fact situation indicates that an express contract existed between the merchant and Alex. In express contracts, the parties make oral or written declarations of their intentions and of the terms of the agreement.

   b. If a contract exists in this situation, it is most likely an implied-in-fact contract. An implied-in-fact contract arises when the parties have expressed assent, but not by written or spoken words. A court in this case could imply such a contract, although the argument for the estate could be that Alex's room and board at the merchant's house was sufficient pay for his work.

   c. An implied-in-law contract arises when the law imposes a contractual obligation because of the parties' relationship or unusual circumstances of the case. This contract can be implied in a parent-child situation, but probably not in this case because the merchant owed no duty to Alex. One could make an argument that equity calls for an implied-in-law contract. However, Alex did receive free room and board. It could be argued that equity does not require additional payment for his work.

2. The contract is valid and binding. Patricia accepted the contract in the manner authorized by Daniel; therefore the acceptance was effective when it left Patricia's control, directed to Daniel.

3. Oliver is not legally bound to Tom, because Tom failed to accept the offer within the period stated. Oliver asked Tom to call him that night, and Tom did not. Oliver could safely assume that Tom did not want the car, even though Oliver did not state the call as a specific condition for keeping the offer open. Therefore, his contract with Oliver's colleague at the office is valid.

4. Sue's lack of capacity to contract based on her minority status may allow her to avoid the contract. The facts do not indicate that Sue's parents were neglectful in providing necessaries for her, so she is probably not liable for the automobile as a necessary. Parents are not usually liable for their children's contracts unless they in some way condone those contracts or direct their formation. In summary, Fred may have no recourse against either Sue or her parents.

Direct Your Learning

Contracts: Consideration and Legal Purpose; Genuine Assent

Educational Objectives

After learning the content of this assignment, you should be able to:

1. Given a case, apply the legal principles governing the types of consideration, the exceptions to the consideration requirement of contract formation, and the adequacy of consideration.

2. Apply legal principles involving contracts that are illegal, narrowly interpreted, or partially enforced.

3. Given a case, apply the elements of fraud to contract formation.

4. Explain how the legal principles of mistake apply to contract formation.

5. Describe the legal principles of each of the following to contract formation:

   a. Duress

   b. Undue influence

   c. Innocent misrepresentation

Study Materials

Required Reading:

▶ The Legal Environment of Insurance
   • Chapter 3

Study Aids:

▶ SMART Online Practice Exams

▶ SMART Study Aids
   • Review Notes and Flash Cards— Assignment 3

Outline

▶ **Third Element of an Enforceable Contract: Consideration**

  A. Types of Consideration

   1. Valuable Consideration

   2. Forbearance

   3. Present, Past, and Future Consideration

   4. Binding Promise

   5. Promise to Perform an Existing Obligation

   6. Compromise and Release of Claims

  B. Adequacy of Consideration

  C. Exceptions to Consideration Requirement

   1. Promissory Estoppel

   2. Charitable Subscriptions

   3. Exceptions Under the UCC

   4. State Statutory Exceptions

  D. Consideration in Insurance Contracts

▶ **Fourth Element of an Enforceable Contract: Legal Purpose**

  A. Types of Illegal Contracts

   1. Contracts to Commit Crimes or Torts

   2. Contracts Harmful to the Public Interest

   3. Usury Contracts

   4. Wagering Contracts

   5. Contracts With Unlicensed Practitioners

   6. Contracts Violating Sunday Laws

   7. Contracts to Transfer Liability for Negligence

   8. Contracts in Restraint of Marriage

   9. Contracts in Restraint of Trade

   10. Unconscionable Bargains

  B. Illegality in Insurance Contracts

   1. Coverage of Contraband

   2. Lack of Insurable Interest

   3. Contracts That Allow an Insured to Profit From Wrong

  C. Qualifications to Illegal Contract Rules

▶ **Genuine Assent**

  A. Fraud

   1. False Representation

   2. Of a Material Fact

   3. Knowingly Made

   4. With Intent to Deceive

   5. On Which the Other Party Has Placed Justifiable Reliance

   6. To His or Her Detriment

   7. Remedies for Fraud

   8. Fraud in Insurance Contracts

  B. Mistake

   1. Unilateral Mistake

   2. Bilateral Mistake

   3. Mistakes in Insurance Contracts

  C. Duress

  D. Undue Influence

  E. Innocent Misrepresentation

▶ **Summary**

Actively capture information by using the open space in the SMART Review Notes to write out key concepts. Putting information into your own words is an effective way to push that information into your memory.

Key Words and Phrases

Define or describe each of the words and phrases listed below.

Valuable consideration (p. 3.4)

Good consideration (p. 3.4)

Gratuitous promise (p. 3.4)

Accord and satisfaction (p. 3.7)

Promissory estoppel (p. 3.9)

Usury (p. 3.12)

Exculpatory clause (p. 3.14)

In pari delicto agreement (p. 3.18)

Severable contract (p. 3.18)

Genuine assent (p. 3.18)

Fraud (p. 3.19)

Rescission (p. 3.22)

Collusion (p. 3.22)

Concealment (p. 3.23)

Mistake (p. 3.26)

Unilateral mistake (p. 3.26)

Bilateral mistake (p. 3.26)

Reformation (p. 3.28)

Duress (p. 3.28)

Undue influence (p. 3.29)

Review Questions

1. What types of consideration can make a promise enforceable? (p. 3.3)

2. In what situations can a debtor's paying only part of a debt be binding on the creditor to forgive the entire debt? (pp. 3.7–3.8)

3. Identify exceptions to the consideration requirement for contracts. (p. 3.8)

4. Distinguish the kind of valuable consideration that will support a property-casualty insurance contract from that which will support a life insurance policy. (pp. 3.10–3.11)

5. List types of illegal contracts. (pp. 3.11–3.16)

6. Are exculpatory clauses always illegal? Explain. (p. 3.14)

7. Under what circumstances are noncompetition agreements valid? (p. 3.15)

8. Give three examples of possible illegality in insurance contracts. (pp. 3.16–3.17)

9. List the conditions under which an illegal contract might still be totally or partially enforceable. (pp. 3.17–3.18)

10. List the situations in which genuine assent to contract may be absent. (pp. 3.18–3.19)

▶▶

11. Explain the material fact element of fraud. (p. 3.20)

12. Describe two situations of fraud in insurance contracts. (pp. 3.22–3.23)

13. Under what circumstances is concealment a defense to an insurance contract? (p. 3.23)

14. Is a unilateral mistake ordinarily a defense to a contract? (pp. 3.26–3.27)

15. What is reformation? (p. 3.28)

16. What effect do mistakes of law have on the binding nature of a contract? (p. 3.28)

17. Under what circumstances may duress permit the avoidance of a contract? (pp. 3.28–3.29)

18. Under what circumstances may undue influence permit the avoidance of a contract? (pp. 3.29–3.30)

19. What is the effect of an innocent misrepresentation relating to a contract? (p. 3.30)

Application Questions

1. Peter and his wife wanted to purchase a house. They had saved the needed 5 percent down payment but hesitated to buy because the monthly payments would be very large. Darrell, Peter's father-in-law, said to Peter, "Son, if you promise to be a good husband to my daughter, I'll give you $10,000 so your payments can come down to a reasonable amount." Peter was elated. He responded affirmatively and with enthusiasm. Two days later, Peter and his wife entered a binding agreement to purchase the house, put down their 5 percent, agreed to pay an additional $10,000 within thirty days, and planned to obtain a mortgage for the balance.

   One week later, Darrell learned that a corporation in which he had invested heavily was bankrupt because of the fraud of its officers. His loss was very large, so he regretfully told his daughter and Peter that he could not go through with his promise. Answer the following questions relating to these facts:

   a. Was there consideration for Darrell's promise? Fully explain what is meant by consideration.

   b. Assuming there is no consideration here, is there any other legal doctrine that might make Darrell's promise binding? Fully explain.

2. Ted, an experienced builder, owned a house and lot situated on a bluff high above Lake Michigan. A few years before the contract in question was made, erosion caused by wind-swept waves started to cause the bluff to collapse and wash away. Ted and his neighbors had unsuccessfully sought government assistance to prevent further erosion. Frank, through a real estate broker, inquired about purchasing Ted's property. Frank asked Ted whether the house was too close to the edge of the bluff and whether the bluff was eroding. Ted replied that he had lived there for many years and that the place was perfectly safe. Frank bought the property, and further erosion during the following year caused the bluff to collapse and disappear completely, taking the house with it. Frank sues Ted for damages. What legal issues are involved?

3. Jill, age seventy, purchased a car on credit and applied for and obtained auto insurance and credit life insurance. In the applications for both policies, Jill listed her age as sixty. While driving the car, Jill suffered a heart attack and died, and the car, out of control, was involved in an accident. Discuss the possible legal consequences, if any, of this misrepresentation on both policies.

4. Stuart has an insurance policy at a premium of $1,295 per year and was shopping around for less expensive coverage. While searching for new coverage, he found three companies that charged approximately the same premium, but a letter from the fourth set a premium of $125. Stuart promptly sent a letter to the fourth company stating, "Please write your policy on the risk we have mentioned and on the terms stated in your recent letter." Discuss the legal principles involved in determining whether the insurer is bound to the $125 premium.

5. Jean, in applying for a life insurance policy, faces three questions she would rather not answer. The first concerns her medical history, which is adverse. The second is whether she has visited a physician within the past five years. She decides to answer the first question untruthfully but tells the agent, truthfully, that she had visited her physician every six months during the past five years. The agent said, "If you want to get the insurance, keep quiet about those visits." The third question refers to drug use. Jean tells the agent that she occasionally smokes marijuana at parties, and the agent replies, "They're not interested in that sort of thing." Are any of the above facts grounds for the insurer to avoid the policy? Explain.

Answers to Assignment 3 Questions

NOTE: These answers are provided to give students a basic understanding of acceptable types of responses. They often are not the only valid answers and are not intended to provide an exhaustive response to the questions.

Review Questions

1. The consideration necessary to make a promise enforceable can be one of the following:
   - A return promise
   - An act performed
   - A forbearance from acting

2. A debtor's paying only part of a debt can be binding on a creditor under the following circumstances:
   - In bona fide disputes when each party agrees to surrender a claim
   - Payment before a debt is due
   - Accord and satisfaction
   - Composition of creditors

3. Exceptions to the consideration requirement include the following:
   - Promissory estoppel
   - Charitable subscriptions
   - Specific exceptions under the UCC provisions
   - State statutory exceptions

4. In property-casualty insurance, prepaying the premium is not a condition necessary to make the contract valid, so that if an insured suffers a loss before paying the premium at the outset of a policy period, an insurer cannot refuse to pay damages based on failure of consideration. However, payment of the entire premium becomes an obligation as soon as the coverage begins. On the other hand, a life insurance policy or application provides that the insurance will not take effect until the purchaser pays the first full premium. Nonpayment can result in forfeiture of policy rights.

5. Types of illegal contracts are as follows:
   - Contracts to commit crimes or torts
   - Contracts harmful to the public interest
   - Usury contracts
   - Wagering contracts
   - Contracts by unlicensed practitioners
   - Contracts violating Sunday laws
   - Contracts attempting to transfer one's negligence liability
   - Contracts restraining marriage
   - Contracts restraining trade
   - Unconscionable bargains

6. Exculpatory clauses are often, but not always, illegal, particularly when a party is at a bargaining disadvantage. Courts interpret them narrowly against the parties attempting to limit their own liability.

7. Noncompetition agreements are valid when they contain restrictions that are necessary to protect the parties and if they impose no undue hardship on the restricted party.

8. Three examples of possible illegality in insurance contracts are as follows:
    (1) The contract covers contraband.
    (2) The insured has no insurable interest in the property or life covered.
    (3) The insured is allowed to profit from his or her wrongful conduct.

9. The conditions under which an illegal contract might still be totally or partially enforceable include the following:
    *   Applicability of protective laws
    *   *In pari delicto* agreements
    *   Severable contracts

10. Genuine assent to contract may be absent in the following situations:
    *   Fraud
    *   Mistake
    *   Duress
    *   Undue influence
    *   Innocent misrepresentation

11. The material fact element of fraud requires that the misleading statement involve a material fact, that is, a fact that a party would consider important in deciding on a course of action.

12. Two situations of fraud in insurance contracts include collusion and concealment. Collusion is an agreement by two or more people to defraud another person. Concealment is misrepresentation by silence.

13. Concealment is a defense to an insurance contract under the following circumstances:
    *   The insured knew that the fact concealed was material.
    *   The insured concealed the fact with the intent to defraud.

14. No, a unilateral mistake is ordinarily not a defense to a contract.

15. Reformation is an equitable remedy with which the court rewrites, or reforms, a contract to reflect the parties' intentions.

16. Mistakes of law, whether unilateral or bilateral, do not affect the binding nature of a contract, particularly when the law is not clear.

17. Duress can permit avoidance of a contract when the wrongdoer deprived the plaintiff of free will in entering the agreement.

18. Undue influence can permit avoidance of a contract when it results in lack of genuine assent to a contract, usually in confidential relationships in which one party exercises some control and influence over the other.

19. If an innocent misrepresentation relates to a material fact and results in a lack of genuine assent, the victim can ask a court to rescind the contract.

Application Questions

1. a. Peter's response that he would be a good husband to Darrell's daughter is a promise to perform an existing obligation because the behavior is an obligation of Peter's marriage. This promise would be insufficient consideration to support a contract.

   b. Darrell's promise is, in effect, a promise to make a gift, or a gratuitous promise. Gratuitous promises are generally unenforceable, but under the doctrine of promissory estoppel, a contract can be enforceable without consideration if the following three elements exist:

      (1) A party makes a promise expecting the other party to act or forbear from acting in reliance on that promise. Darrell expected Peter and his wife to purchase the house in reliance on receiving his gift of $10,000.

      (2) The other party justifiably relies on the promise by acting or forbearing from acting. Peter and his wife acted on Darrell's promise when they contracted to buy the house.

      (3) Only enforcement of the promise will achieve justice, and that is probably the case in this situation.

2. The legal issues raised by the case include the following:

   • Did genuine assent exist in this agreement?

   • Was there fraud?

   • Is Ted liable to Frank?

   • Is the broker liable to Frank?

   • What damages may Frank seek?

   Did you see any other issues?

3. Jill's misrepresentation of her age may not be material to the auto policy. It is difficult to predict whether a seventy-year-old has a higher risk of accidents under an auto policy than a sixty-year-old. (Studies probably vary on this issue.) On the other hand, age is material in life insurance with regard to mortality rates, and Jill's misrepresentation may permit the insurer to avoid the policy.

4. This case involves a mistake by the insurer on its correspondence, and the mistake should be obvious to Stuart. When an offeree knows or has reason to know that an offer is a mistake, the offeree may not profit by taking advantage of the offer. The company should not be bound to the premium.

5. a. Jean's medical history—Jean's misrepresentation is material in a life insurance policy application and may be grounds for avoidance.

   b. Jean's physician visits—Both the agent and Jean have made a misrepresentation, which may be material in this life insurance contract and may be grounds for avoidance.

   c. Jean's occasional marijuana use—The application asks about drug use, and even casual use of a drug may be material on a life insurance application. This misrepresentation could also be grounds for avoidance if it proves to increase the risk on the policy.

Direct Your Learning

Contracts: Form, Interpretation, and Obligations

Educational Objectives

After learning the content of this assignment, you should be able to:

1. Explain whether the statute of frauds would apply in a case.

2. Explain whether the parol evidence rule would apply in a case.

3. Apply contractual rules of interpretation in a case.

4. Describe the types of rights that are assignable and the rights of the respective parties in an assignment.

5. Describe the rights of third-party beneficiaries in a case.

6. Explain whether discharge of contract by performance, new agreement, or impossibility has occurred in a case.

7. Explain how the three types of contractual conditions apply in a case.

8. Describe breach of contract and types of remedies available for breach in a case.

Study Materials

Required Reading:
▶ The Legal Environment of Insurance
  • Chapter 4

Study Aids:
▶ SMART Online Practice Exams
▶ SMART Study Aids
  • Review Notes and Flash Cards—Assignment 4

Outline

▶ **Statute of Frauds**

  A. Contracts Requiring Writing

    1. Contracts for the Sale of Land

    2. Contracts That Cannot Be Performed Within One Year

    3. Contracts to Pay Another's Debt

    4. Contracts in Consideration of Marriage

    5. Contracts to Pay Estate Debts From Executor's Funds

    6. Contracts for Sale of Personal Property for $500 or More

  B. Form Required

  C. Insurance Contracts

    1. Performance Within a Year

    2. Another's Debt

▶ **Parol Evidence Rule**

  A. Exceptions to the Parol Evidence Rule

    1. Incomplete Contracts

    2. Ambiguity

    3. Fraud, Accident, Illegality, or Mistake

    4. Condition Precedent

    5. Parol Evidence and UCC

▶ **Contract Interpretation**

  A. Plain Meaning

  B. Effectuation of Intent

  C. Entire and Divisible Contracts

  D. Clerical Errors and Omissions

  E. Contradictory Terms

  F. Ambiguity

  G. Parties' Own Interpretation

  H. Legal and Fair Interpretations

  I. Trade Usage, Course of Dealings, and Performance

▶ **Third-Party Rights**

  A. Contract Assignments

    1. Rights Assignable

    2. Rights Not Assignable

    3. Assignment and the UCC

    4. Forms of Assignment

    5. Consideration

    6. Assignee's Rights

    7. Assignee's Duties

    8. Notice of Assignment

  B. Third-Party Beneficiaries

    1. Types of Beneficiaries

    2. Characteristics of Beneficiary Contracts

    3. Beneficiaries' Rights

▶ **Discharge of Contracts**

  A. Performance

    1. Payment

    2. Tender of Performance

    3. Substantial Performance

    4. Personal Satisfaction

    5. Agreed Time

  B. Agreement of the Parties

  C. Substitution

  D. Impossibility

    1. Causes of Impossibility

    2. Temporary and Partial Impossibility and Partial Performance

    3. Frustration of Purpose

    4. Commercial Impracticability

    5. Statutes of Limitations

    6. Fraudulent Alteration

▶ **Conditions**

▶ **Breach of Contract**

  A. Types of Breach

    1. Repudiation

    2. Anticipatory Breach

    3. Material Breach

  B. Remedies for Breach

    1. Damages

    2. Action for Price

    3. Equitable Remedies

▶ **Summary**

Key Words and Phrases

Define or describe each of the words and phrases listed below.

Statute of frauds (p. 4.3)

Executor (p. 4.7)

Administrator (p. 4.7)

Parol evidence rule (p. 4.11)

Assignment (p. 4.20)

Assignor (p. 4.20)

Assignee (p. 4.20)

Third-party beneficiary contract (p. 4.25)

Creditor beneficiary (p. 4.25)

Donee beneficiary (p. 4.25)

Incidental beneficiary (p. 4.25)

Intended beneficiary (p. 4.25)

Tender (p. 4.28)

Novation (p. 4.30)

Condition precedent (p. 4.35)

Condition concurrent (p. 4.35)

Condition subsequent (p. 4.35)

Repudiation (p. 4.36)

Anticipatory breach (p. 4.36)

▶▶

Compensatory damages (p. 4.38)

Consequential damages (p. 4.38)

Punitive, or exemplary damages (p. 4.39)

Extracontractual damages (p. 4.39)

Mitigation of damages (p. 4.39)

Liquidated damages (p. 4.40)

Specific performance (p. 4.41)

Injunction (p. 4.41)

Reformation (p. 4.42)

Review Questions

1. Identify the situations in which a contract must be in writing under the statute of frauds. (p. 4.4)

2. Under what circumstances, if any, will an oral executory contract to sell a house and land be legally enforceable? (pp. 4.4–4.5)

3. How have courts interpreted the statute of frauds with regard to contracts that cannot be performed in a year? (pp. 4.5–4.6)

4. For sale of personal property under the UCC, what terms must a contract contain to satisfy the statute of frauds? (p. 4.8)

5. What type of writing is sufficient to satisfy the statute of frauds? (p. 4.9)

6. What insurance contracts, if any, are subject to the statute of frauds? (p. 4.10)

7. What is the purpose and effect of the parol evidence rule? (p. 4.11)

8. Describe the exceptions to the parol evidence rule. (pp. 4.12–4.13)

9. What is a court's goal in interpreting a contract? (p. 4.14)

10. Describe the effect of treating contracts as divisible. (pp. 4.15–4.16)

11. Under the UCC, how will a court enforce a contract for the sale of goods when the contract does not contain the price of goods sold? (p. 4.17)

12. What guidelines do courts use to resolve contradictory terms? (pp. 4.17–4.18)

13. How do courts resolve ambiguous contractual terms? (p. 4.18)

14. How does the UCC reconcile conflicts among the following: (p. 4.20)
    a. The express terms of an agreement
    b. Trade usage
    c. Course of dealing between the parties
    d. Course of performance between the parties

15. State the types of situations in which rights may not be assigned. (p. 4.21)

16. Explain why an assignee of a debt should immediately notify the obligor of the assignment? (p. 4.24)

17. In the absence of a provision in the contract to the contrary, may the original parties to a contract cut off the rights of a third-party beneficiary without the consent of the beneficiary? (p. 4.26)

18. Why do courts recognize substantial performance that falls short of actual performance? (pp. 4.28–4.29)

19. What is the effect of a contract provision that requires performance by a certain date and states that time is "of the essence" in this agreement? (p. 4.29)

20. Explain how one agreement can discharge contractual obligations under another agreement. (p. 4.31)

21. Identify four changes in circumstances that make performance of a contract impossible. (p. 4.32)

22. Discuss the relationship of increased cost to commercial impracticability. (p. 4.34)

23. What is the purpose of the doctrine of anticipatory breach? (p. 4.37)

24. What are the effects of a minor breach of contract? (p. 4.37)

25. When does a court award consequential damages for breach of contract? (p. 4.39)

26. When does a court award extracontractual damages against insurers? (pp. 4.39–4.40)

27. Under what circumstances do courts order equitable remedies? (pp. 4.40–4.41)

Application Questions

1. Barry has been negotiating for the purchase of Sam's house. They haggled for over three months and finally agreed on a price of $200,000. Sam's lawyer prepared an agreement that merely stated that the property was to be conveyed at that price within ninety days. At the closing, Barry inquires about the patio furniture and the microwave. Sam says they were not included. Barry produces a letter from Sam dated two months prior to the final agreement, stating that the patio furniture would go with the house. Barry maintains vehemently that Sam also orally agreed, at the time of the signing of the agreement, that the microwave would go with the house.

   a. On what legal basis will the letter and conversation be excluded as evidence? Fully explain.

   b. What does Barry need to allege and prove to have such evidence admitted? Fully explain.

2. Charles had a judgment of $5,000 against Dianne and was about to bring legal proceedings to attach Dianne's machinery for the debt. Frank was also a creditor of Dianne's for a much greater amount and feared that, if Charles attached Dianne's machinery, it would halt Dianne's business and, as a result, Dianne would not be able to pay Frank. Frank wants Charles not to proceed with the attachment and is willing to guarantee the payment of Dianne's debt to achieve that objective. Must the agreement between Frank and Charles be in writing to be legally enforceable? Why or why not?

3. Eric was employed as a sales manager by Cosmetics Corporation. He approached the president of Beauty-Smart Company for a new position. On December 16, the president of Beauty-Smart told Eric that, if he would come to work for Beauty-Smart as a sales manager on January 1, and if his work is satisfactory for a full twelve months, he would be paid $60,000 the following January 15. Eric agreed to these terms, quit his job with Cosmetics, and went to work for Beauty-Smart. After working there for nine months, he was unjustly dismissed.

   a. Eric sues Beauty-Smart for breach of contract. Is he entitled to recover? Explain.

   b. Assume that the parties agreed orally that Eric was to have employment with Beauty-Smart for life. Would the contract be enforceable? Explain.

4. Buyer sues Seller for damages for an alleged breach of contract for 300 barrels of furniture oil, claiming that the oil was not up to the special specifications required. The written contract merely called for "300 barrels of furniture oil," and Buyer wants to introduce evidence to prove that prior contracts with Seller, which were fully performed, were for oil with specifications. Buyer also wants to introduce into evidence the letter of inquiry that led to the current contract and that expressed interest in contracting for "another 300 barrels of the special furniture oil you have delivered in the past." Seller objects to the introduction of either type of evidence on the ground that introduction will be contrary to the parol evidence rule. Seller, in turn, wishes to introduce evidence of the generally accepted meaning of "furniture oil" in the trade, and Buyer objects to the admission of that evidence. Comment on the admissibility of the evidence of the letter, prior course dealings, and trade usage, and on the effect of the Uniform Commercial Code on this problem.

5. Jerry had a contract to construct a certain building for Maggie. Jerry entered into a contract with X Bank to finance that specific project and entered into contracts with various subcontractors to do the work. After the subcontractors had completed various portions of their work, X Bank refused to honor its agreement to lend Jerry the money. As a result, Jerry could not pay the subcontractors. The subcontractors now sue X Bank, claiming they are third-party beneficiaries under the bank's contract with Jerry. Are they? Explain.

▶▶

Answers to Assignment 4 Questions

NOTE: These answers are provided to give students a basic understanding of acceptable types of responses. They often are not the only valid answers and are not intended to provide an exhaustive response to the questions.

Review Questions

1. The situations in which a contract must be in writing under the statute of frauds are the following:
   - Contracts for the sale of land or any interest in land
   - Contracts that cannot be performed within one year
   - Promises to pay another's debt
   - Promises in consideration of marriage
   - Promises by executors of decedents' estates to pay estate debts from executors' own funds
   - Contracts involving sale of personal property for $500 or more

2. When the purchaser of real property has taken possession of the property and made substantial improvements in reliance on an oral contract to sell, most courts enforce the oral contract.

3. Courts have not favored the one-year requirement and generally hold the provision requiring written contracts inapplicable if it is possible to perform the contract within one year.

4. A contract for the sale of personal property must contain terms relating to the quantity of goods for sale to satisfy the statute of frauds.

5. To satisfy the statute of frauds, a written note or memorandum is sufficient.

6. Of the six situations to which the statute of frauds applies, courts have considered applying only two to insurance contracts: (1) policies that are contracts that cannot be performed within one year and (2) policies that are promises to answer for another's debt.

7. The parol evidence rule, which limits the terms of a contract to those expressed in writing, has the following three purposes: (1) to carry out the parties' presumed intentions, (2) to achieve certainty and finality as to the parties' rights and duties, and (3) to exclude fraudulent and perjured claims.

8. Parol evidence is allowed under the following circumstances:
   - To prove terms of incomplete contracts
   - To clarify ambiguity in a contract
   - To support an allegation of fraud, accident, illegality, or mistake relating to a contract
   - To prove failure of a condition precedent

9. A court's goal in interpreting a contract is to determine the intentions of the parties.

10. The effect of treating contracts as divisible is that the performance of a portion of the contract entitles the performing party to immediate payment.

11. If the parties fail to state a price for the goods, a court will assume that the contract implies a reasonable price.

12. To resolve contradictory terms, the courts apply a system of priorities:
    - Handwriting prevails over typewriting.
    - Typewriting prevails over printing.
    - Words prevail over figures.

13. If a provision can have more than one reasonable meaning, the courts adopt the interpretation least favorable to the party who put the provision into the contract and most favorable for the party who assented to it. If a provision is so ambiguous that its meaning cannot be determined with the usual tools of interpretation, the court can admit evidence from outside the contract.

14. The UCC reconciles conflicts by establishing the following priorities when these considerations are in conflict: (a) express terms of the contract, (b) course of performance, (c) course of dealings, and (d) trade usage.

15. The following are the most common situations in which contract rights are not assignable:
    - Legal restrictions
    - Contract restrictions
    - Personal contracts
    - Alteration of performance
    - Personal satisfaction contracts
    - Damages for personal injury

16. The assignee should notify the obligor of the assignment to ensure that the obligor pays the assignee rather than the assignor, thus defeating the original assignor's right to demand the obligor's payment or performance.

17. The modern legal trend is to permit the original parties in all cases to cut off the beneficiaries' rights unless beneficiaries can prove that their positions have changed materially in reasonable reliance on the contracts.

18. Rather than permit the promisee to escape liability completely on the ground of nonperformance, courts consider whether the performance actually given was substantial performance and whether the party performed in good faith.

19. If a contract provision requires performance by a certain date and states that "time is of the essence in this agreement," then a court will enforce that provision.

20. Contractual obligations can be discharged by another agreement by accord and satisfaction, the substitution of a different performance for the performance required in a contract.

21. The following are four changes in circumstances that make performance of a contract impossible:
    (1) Change in law
    (2) Death or incapacity
    (3) Destruction of subject matter
    (4) Other party's act

22. Increased cost can constitute commercial impracticability if the increase is drastic. However, even in this case, the seller must take commercially reasonable precautions to protect the source of supply.

23. The concept of anticipatory breach developed to avoid "enforced idleness" on the part of the aggrieved party, who must wait until the time of performance to sue for breach, and to make it unnecessary for that party to tender performance at the time stated in the contract to prove the other party's breach.

24. The effects of a "minor" breach of contract include the following:
    - It temporarily suspends any duty of performance by the nonbreaching party that would have arisen on proper performance.
    - It gives the aggrieved party a basis to sue for damages for the breach—usually an offset to the agreed price—but not for remedies for breach of the entire contract.

25. Consequential damages are awarded to the plaintiff only when the defendant was aware of the probable occurrence of the damages.

26. Courts award extracontractual damages against insurers on the following grounds:
    - Breach of the insurer's duty of good faith and fair dealing in insurance contracts
    - Intentional infliction of emotional distress on the insured by the insurer's extreme and outrageous conduct

27. Courts order equitable remedies under the following circumstances:
    - When the buyer has accepted the goods
    - When a carrier has tendered the goods to the buyer if the contract requires the seller to ship them to the buyer
    - When the seller has delivered the goods to the carrier if the contract provides only for delivery to the carrier and not to the destination
    - When a third party holds the goods for delivery without moving them
    - When the buyer has received a document indicating the buyer's right to the goods
    - When the third party acknowledges the buyer's right to possession

Application Questions

1. a. A real estate contract is a formal agreement and must be in writing under the statute of frauds. The parol evidence rule limits the terms of a contract to those expressed in writing. It prevents the introduction of any oral or written evidence of an agreement, including letters and conversations. This rule would exclude the evidence in question.

   b. Barry would have to prove that the contract was incomplete, or ambiguous; that it was the result of fraud, accident, illegality, or mistake; or that a condition precedent failed to occur.

2. Frank has agreed to pay Dianne's debt to achieve his objective to collect his own debt from her. Ordinarily, an agreement to pay another's debt must be in writing under the statute of frauds. However, when the primary purpose is to achieve the promisor's own business purpose, the agreements need not be in writing to be enforceable.

3. a. Because this contract could be performed within one year, a writing was not necessary under the statute of frauds. Eric performed his part of the agreement, but Beauty Smart Company was in breach. As a matter of fairness, however, a court would allow Eric to recover any damages.

b. A contract for employment for life appears to require a writing because it can involve performance beyond a year. However, courts do not favor the one-year requirement for a writing and generally hold the provision inapplicable if it is possible to perform the agreement within one year. Here, for example, Eric's life, and thus, his employment, could end within one year, taking his agreement out of the statute of frauds.

4. The UCC provides that the contract writing need not set forth all the material terms of the contract to be binding. The letter is allowable evidence to show that the written contract was not the entire agreement and that the letter further explains the agreement in question. The only term required in the basic written agreement is the quantity, which need not be stated accurately. The UCC recognizes the parol evidence rule but allows for evidence of a prior course of dealings between the parties—which would allow admission of Buyer's evidence—as well as evidence of trade usage, which would allow admission of Seller's evidence.

5. This case could have several answers. For example, a third-party beneficiary contract is a contract between two parties that benefits a third party, either directly or indirectly. In this situation, Jerry and X Bank are the two contracting parties, and the subcontractors are beneficiaries of that contract. Because financing a project through a bank directly benefits any subcontractors who must be paid via that financing, the subcontractors are direct beneficiaries. Financing the project would allow Jerry to discharge obligations owed, such as those to subcontractors, so they could be creditor beneficiaries in this case. The following are notable characteristics of beneficiary contracts:

- A binding contract must exist between the promisor and the promisee.
- The parties to the contract must intend that the third party benefit by and acquire rights under the contract. No gift is involved here, and creditor beneficiary is the category that probably fits best.
- Clarifying to whom performance is due is necessary. Financing of a project means giving the project owner the ability to pay—including the ability to pay subcontractors. In this case, therefore, arguably, performance is due the subcontractors. However, the bank might argue that it would owe performance only to Jerry, and that, therefore, only Jerry can sue.

Use the SMART Online Practice Exams to test your understanding of the course material. You can review questions over a single assignment or multiple assignments, or you can take an exam over the entire course. The questions are scored, and you are shown your results. (You score essay exams yourself.)

Direct Your Learning

Insurance Contract Law

Educational Objectives

After learning the content of this assignment, you should be able to:

1. Describe the following characteristics of insurance contracts:

    a. A conditional contract

    b. A contract involving fortuitous events and the exchange of unequal amounts

    c. A contract of utmost good faith

    d. A contract of adhesion

    e. A contract of indemnity

    f. A nontransferable contract

2. Given a case, determine whether an insurance contract has formed based on the elements of insurance contracts.

3. Given a case involving third-party interests, determine how an insurance policy can provide coverage.

4. Evaluate a representation in an insurance application to determine whether a misrepresentation has occurred.

5. Explain the effects of warranties in an insurance contract case.

6. Explain how insurers can waive their rights or face estoppel from asserting their rights against their insureds.

7. Explain how reservation of rights letters and nonwaiver agreements affect insurers' and insureds' rights.

Study Materials

Required Reading:
▶ The Legal Environment of Insurance
  • Chapter 5

Study Aids:
▶ SMART Online Practice Exams
▶ SMART Study Aids
  • Review Notes and Flash Cards—Assignment 5

Outline

▶ **Special Characteristics of Insurance Contracts**

   A. Conditional Contract

   B. Contract Involving Fortuitous Events and the Exchange of Unequal Amounts

   C. Contract of Utmost Good Faith

      1. Concealment

      2. Misrepresentation

   D. Contract of Adhesion

   E. Contract of Indemnity

   F. Nontransferable Contract

▶ **Insurance Contract Elements**

   A. Agreement

      1. Offer and Acceptance

      2. Effective Date

      3. Silence or Delay

   B. Insurance Policy Content

   C. Written Versus Oral and Informal Written Contracts

      1. Oral Insurance Contracts

      2. Necessary Terms

      3. Implied Terms

      4. Insurance Company Designation

   D. Delivery of Insurance Policies

      1. Constructive Delivery

      2. Conditional Receipts

      3. First Premium Payment

▶ **Insurance as Third-Party Beneficiary Contract**

   A. Third-Party Interests in Liability Insurance

   B. Real Estate Sellers and Buyers

   C. Mortgagor's and Mortgagee's Interests

   D. Limited Interests in Realty

      1. Lease Interests

      2. Life Estates

   E. Sellers and Buyers of Goods

▶ **Representations and Warranties in Insurance**

   A. Representations

      1. False or Misleading Statement

      2. Material Fact

      3. Reliance on False or Misleading Statements

      4. Statutory Approaches to Misrepresentation

      5. Construction of Representations

   B. Warranties

      1. Distinguished From Representation

      2. Incontestable Clause

      3. Classification

      4. Lessening Warranty Effects

▶ **Waiver, Estoppel, and Election**

   A. Waiver

      1. Use of Waivers

      2. Consideration

      3. Knowledge Requirement

      4. Policy Provisions

      5. Acts Constituting Waiver

      6. Parol Evidence Rule

   B. Estoppel

      1. Insurance Law and Estoppel

      2. Distinguishing Estoppel From Waiver

      3. Factors Establishing Estoppel

   C. Election

      1. Application

      2. Insured's Election

   D. Choosing Among Waiver, Estoppel, and Election

   E. Insurer's Protection Against Waiver, Estoppel, and Election

      1. Justified Refusal

      2. Unjustified Refusal

      3. Reservation of Rights Notice or Nonwaiver Agreement

▶ **Summary**

Key Words and Phrases

Define or describe each of the words and phrases listed below.

Insurance policy (p. 5.3)

Conditional contract (p. 5.4)

Utmost good faith (p. 5.5)

Material fact (p. 5.6)

Misrepresentation (p. 5.6)

Contract of adhesion (p. 5.7)

Contract of indemnity (p. 5.7)

Principle of indemnity (p. 5.8)

Valued policy (p. 5.8)

Binder (p. 5.12)

Conditional receipt (p. 5.13)

Binding receipt (p. 5.13)

Approval receipt (p. 5.13)

Insurability receipt (p. 5.14)

Direct-action statute (p. 5.22)

Incontestable clause (p. 5.29)

Contestable period (p. 5.30)

Warranty (p. 5.32)

Affirmative warranty (p. 5.32)

Continuing, or promissory, warranty (p. 5.32)

Implied warranty (p. 5.32)

Waiver (p. 5.34)

Estoppel (p. 5.37)

Election (p. 5.40)

Nonwaiver agreement (p. 5.43)

Reservation of rights letter (p. 5.43)

Review Questions

1. What basic rule of construction do courts use in interpreting contracts of adhesion? (p. 5.7)

2. What three tasks do agents usually perform for insurers? (p. 5.9)

3. Explain under what circumstances an issued policy might be merely an offer. (p. 5.10)

4. When do parties make the offer and acceptance to form a life insurance contract? (p. 5.11)

5. What essential information must a binder contain for property-casualty insurance? (p. 5.13)

6. To what terms must parties agree to have a valid oral or informal insurance policy? (pp. 5.18–5.19)

7. Explain what contractual terms parties might imply and how courts determine those terms in case of an incomplete agreement. (p. 5.18)

8. Explain why claimants under liability policies are not considered third-party beneficiaries in states that have not adopted direct action statutes. (p. 5.22)

9. Why does a buyer of real estate under an incomplete agreement of sale need insurance? (pp. 5.22–5.23)

10. Does a buyer of undelivered goods face the same exposure as a buyer of real estate? (pp. 5.24–5.25)

11. What is the effect of a policyholder's misrepresentation? (pp. 5.26–5.27)

12. What determines whether a fact is material? (p. 5.27)

13. Explain why contribute-to-loss statutes create a more difficult standard for an insurer to show materiality sufficient to avoid a contract than do increase-of-risk statutes. (p. 5.28)

14. State the two requirements for a promise or stipulation to be a warranty in an insurance policy. (p. 5.29)

15. Explain how warranties differ from representations. (p. 5.29)

16. Explain the purpose and effect of the incontestable clause in life, accident, and health insurance policies. (pp. 5.29–5.31)

17. How has the law lessened warranty effects? (p. 5.33)

18. What are the requirements for a waiver? (p. 5.34)

19. Must consideration support waivers of insurance policy provisions? (p. 5.35)

20. State the requisites of estoppel in insurance law. (pp. 5.37–5.38)

21. Distinguish waiver from estoppel. (p. 5.38)

22. What is the effect of an election? (p. 5.40)

23. Explain the purpose and form of a nonwaiver agreement and a reservation of rights notice. (pp. 5.43–5.44)

Application Questions

1. Louise ordered a life insurance policy and received an "insurability receipt" in return for the premium. Before Louise was to take a medical examination, she died in an accident. The insurer offers to return the premium paid, and Louise's estate demands the policy limits. What steps are necessary to determine the insurer's liability?

2. Yates has purchased all his property and liability policies from Omega Insurance Company through Al's Agency, which represents Omega, Pine, and Maple Insurance Companies. Al's Agency, having learned that Yates had purchased a boat, mails Yates a letter suggesting insuring the boat for $10,000 and quotes the premium for this coverage. Yates, before receiving that letter, and wanting to protect his new boat, writes Al's Agency requesting $10,000 of boat insurance and offers to pay whatever the premium might be. Yates's boat sustains a fire loss before either party receives either letter.

   a. Is Yates's loss covered? Why or why not?

b. Assuming that Al's Agency has received Yates's letter before the fire and that it has not started to process his application, which, if any, of the three insurers is liable for the loss? Explain.

3. Don has moved into a large farmhouse. He calls the Alert Agency and asks how much insurance he needs on the house. Agent states he would need $150,000 of insurance and the premium would be about $500. Don asks Agent to obtain a property insurance policy for him. Agent agrees to secure a policy from the insurer offering the best rate and service. The agency represents several insurers. That night, Don's home burns down.

a. Using the information given, explain the terms to which the parties must agree to create an insurance contract.

b. If Agent had contacted no insurers, but generally placed farm properties in the Shieldgard Insurance Company, could Don sue anyone?

    c.   Assume, for the purpose of the subpart, that Agent wrote herself a note, saying "Place Don's house in Shieldgard," but had not notified Shieldgard prior to the fire. Would this information change your answer to the previous question? Explain.

4. Jim is about to purchase a house. Jim's friend Anne tells him to obtain a fire insurance policy on the house to be effective as soon as the binding agreement is signed. Jim says, "Nonsense! Why should I pay a premium when the house is still the seller's until I get the deed? I bought an $800 television set a few months ago, and a store fire completely burned it. The store had to deliver another one just like it to me because the fire was their problem, not mine!" Comment on the accuracy of both of Jim's statements.

Answers to Assignment 5 Questions

NOTE: These answers are provided to give students a basic understanding of acceptable types of responses. They often are not the only valid answers and are not intended to provide an exhaustive response to the questions.

Review Questions

1. If the contract's wording is ambiguous, a court will generally apply the interpretation that favors the insured.

2. Three tasks the insurance agent performs for insurers is to solicit business, take applications, and sometimes issue policies.

3. If the policy as issued does not comply with the coverage or rates the applicant requested, the policy is a new offer that the applicant can accept or reject.

4. In the life insurance contract, the prospective insured offers to contract by submitting an application. Acceptance of the offer and formation of the contract are not effective under most life insurance policies until actual delivery of the policy to the insured and payment of the first premium.

5. Property-casualty insurance binders must contain the basic information needed for an agreement, such as identification of the insurer and the insured and a description of the insured property, and must indicate types and amounts of coverage clearly enough to establish policy limits.

6. The terms to which parties must agree to have a valid oral or informal insurance policy include the following:
   - The types of coverage sought
   - The object or premises, if any, to be insured
   - The amount of insurance
   - The insured's name
   - The duration of coverage

7. Terms that might be implied and how they are determined are as follows:
   - The type of policy, based on the type an insurer usually issues in a given situation or the type of policy most insurers usually issue
   - The provisions of a policy, based on policies the insurer customarily issues
   - A policy premium, based on the rate the insurer has filed with the insurance regulatory authorities in cases in which the parties have not specified the premium amount and the insurer and insured have had no previous dealings
   - The insured's coverage needs, based on comparisons with the coverage needs of others engaged in similar endeavors

8. Claimants under liability policies can benefit from liability insurance. However, in states without direct-action statutes, victims cannot sue a wrongdoer's insurer directly until a court orders a judgment against the insured. In these states the purpose of liability insurance is to indemnify the insured for losses in paying damages.

9. A buyer of real estate under an incomplete agreement of sale needs insurance because the buyer bears the risk of loss under the doctrine of equitable conversion, even before the time of the actual title transfer.

10. A buyer of undelivered goods does not face the same exposure as a buyer of real estate because the doctrine of equitable conversion applies only to real estate. The seller of the goods assumes all chance of loss until the buyer either receives or refuses to accept those goods.

11. The effect of a policyholder's misrepresentation is to make the insurance contract voidable.

12. The test for material fact is whether the insurer was influenced or induced to enter into the contract in reliance on the representation.

13. Increase-of-risk statutes set either objective or subjective standards for determining materiality. Under contribute-to-loss statutes, regardless of materiality, a misrepresentation does not allow an insurer to avoid the contract if, from its very nature, the misrepresentation could not contribute to the destruction of the property.

14. For a promise to be a warranty, the following two requirements must be present:
    (1) The parties must have clearly and unmistakably intended it to be a warranty.
    (2) The statement must form a part of the contract itself.

15. Warranties differ from representations as follows:
    *   Warranties are part of the final insurance contract. Representations are merely collateral inducements to the contract.
    *   The law presumes warranties to be material, and their breach makes the contract voidable. To constitute a valid defense, representations must be proven to be material.
    *   Warranties are either written in the policy or incorporated by reference. Representations can be oral, written in the policy, or written in another document and incorporated by reference into the policy.
    *   Warranties require strict compliance. Representations require substantial truth only.

16. Incontestable clauses assure life, accident, and health insurance policyholders that their beneficiaries will receive payment. An insurer cannot assert material misrepresentation, concealment, or fraud in connection with life insurance applications when the policy has been in force longer than the contestable period during the insured's life.

17. The law has lessened warranty effects in the following ways:
    *   By interpreting warranties as affirmative rather than as continuing
    *   By interpreting policies as severable
    *   By not considering the use of the word "warranty" as conclusive
    *   By making a breach of warranty no more burdensome for the insured or beneficiary than a material false representation
    *   By preventing insurers from specifying that representations have the same effect as warranties

18. The requirements for a waiver are that an insurance policy must exist and that an insurer must know of a breach of condition under the policy before it can waive that condition.

19. In insurance law, some waivers are binding without consideration, such as when an insurer pays for a loss after the policy period for filing proof of loss has elapsed and without having received proof of loss.

20. The requisites of estoppel in insurance law are:
    - False representation of a material fact
    - Reasonable reliance on the representation
    - Resulting injury or detriment to the insured

21. Waiver differs from estoppel in the following ways:
    - Waiver is contractual and rests upon agreement between parties. Estoppel is equitable and arises from false representation.
    - Waiver gives effect to the waiving party's intention. Estoppel defeats the inequitable intent of the estopped party.
    - The parol evidence rule applies to waiver but not to estoppel.

22. The effect of an election is that a choice of one available right implies a relinquishment of the right not chosen.

23. Insurers use nonwaiver agreements and reservation of rights notices to preserve certain defenses against liability that they might have had under policy terms. A reservation of rights letter is usually in the form of a unilateral notice, usually a letter from the insurer to the insured. A nonwaiver agreement is in the form of a document in which the insured and the insurer agree that neither will waive any of its rights under the policy resulting from the investigation or defense of a lawsuit against the insured.

Application Questions

1. Typically, an insurability receipt states that the insurance is effective on the date of the receipt or on the date of the medical examination, provided the applicant is insurable on that date. Louise died before having a medical examination. If the insurability receipt says the insurance was effective on the date of the receipt, Louise's estate receives her insurance proceeds. On the other hand, if the insurability receipt says that the insurance was to be effective upon a favorable medical examination, then an investigation might be ordered to determine whether Louise would have met underwriting standards on the date of the medical examination.

2. a. Yates's loss is not covered. Al's Agency's initial letter suggests that Yates obtain the $10,000 in coverage and quotes a premium. Yates writes a letter that crosses in the mail with Al's Agency's letter. In effect, two offers are made, but no acceptances occur, so no agreement has resulted.

   b. Assuming that Al's Agency received Yates's letter and that the agency had not started to process the application, no liability would arise unless either the insurer or the agent was negligent in delaying the application processing. There is no evidence indicating that any insurer is preferred for this policy, although past practices indicate that Omega would be the assumed insurer in the absence of evidence to the contrary.

3. a. Don's agreement to insure must contain the following:

*   Types of coverage—Standard coverages would probably apply.

*   Risks or events insured against—Again, the assumption is standard risks/events.

*   The premises and/or objects to be insured—Don lives in the farmhouse, and he has requested coverage for the farmhouse.

*   Type of liability insurance, if any—The assumption is that Agent is providing standard coverage.

*   Reasonable identification—If Don lives in only one farmhouse, this identification is sufficient.

*   Amount of insurance—It is $150,000.

*   Insured's name—Don identifies himself.

*   The duration of the coverage (even if only by implication)—This is not clear, but Don's farmhouse burns down that night. Any period would be longer than a few hours.

It is difficult to determine whether coverage is in effect. We have no information as to an oral binder to that effect.

b. There is no evidence of any previous dealings between Don and Alert that would give rise to a presumption about any particular insurer. However, if Alert generally uses Shieldgard for farm companies, and if the rate of $500 quoted by Alert is one Shieldgard would provide, it might be safe to assume that Shieldgard is the intended insurer. If an insurance contract exists, Don could sue Shieldgard.

c. A note could resolve this issue and could bind Shieldgard, so that Don could sue Shieldgard. This does not change the answer to the previous question.

4. First, rules applicable to real estate do not necessarily apply to goods, and vice versa. Even after full payment of the purchase price, a seller of goods who keeps possession assumes responsibility for the risk of loss until after the buyer either receives the goods or refuses to accept them. Whether Jim had paid for the television set is still not clear, but it does not matter. The store still bore the risk of loss.

In the case of the house, Jim as the buyer would have an equitable interest in the house when the agreement of sale is signed. However, no binding agreement has been signed. Thus, Jim is probably correct that he does not need the insurance now. However, he should insure the house when a binding agreement of sale is signed. Jim is incorrect about waiting to get the deed unless he and the seller also agree that the seller bears the entire risk until final transfer of the property to Jim. In the absence of such an agreement, Jim should obtain insurance as soon as the agreement of sale is signed. At the very least, he should make sure the seller has insurance coverage that would protect his interests as well.

The SMART Online Practice Exams product contains a final practice exam. You should take this exam only when you have completed your study of the entire course. Take this exam under simulated exam conditions. It will be your best indicator of how well prepared you are.

Direct Your Learning

Commercial Law

Educational Objectives

After learning the content of this assignment, you should be able to:

1. Regarding sales contracts, describe the following:

    a. Rules of contract law applying to the sale of goods

    b. Warranties made in sales of goods

    c. Types of sales contracts

    d. Delivery terms

2. Given a case, explain what risk of loss each party to a sales transaction bears.

3. Given a case, explain whether and why a breach of sales agreement occurs and what remedies buyers and sellers have.

4. Explain what legal principles apply to the following:

    a. Commercial paper

    b. Elements of negotiability

    c. Transfer and negotiation

    d. Holders in due course

    e. Checks

    f. Security interests

5. Explain how provisions relating to the following apply in a case:

    a. Fair trade laws

    b. Consumer warranty laws

    c. Consumer credit laws

    d. Bankruptcy

Study Materials

Required Reading:
▶ The Legal Environment of Insurance
  • Chapter 6

Study Aids:
▶ SMART Online Practice Exams
▶ SMART Study Aids
  • Review Notes and Flash Cards— Assignment 6

Outline

▶ **Sales Contracts (UCC Article 2)**
  A. General Contract Law Application
    1. Offer and Acceptance
    2. Consideration
  B. Warranties
    1. Express Warranties
    2. Implied Warranties
    3. Third-Party Beneficiaries of Warranties
  C. Types of Sales Contracts
  D. Delivery Terms, Inspection, and Time
    1. Inspection
    2. Time for Delivery
  E. Title and Risk of Loss
  F. Breach of Sales Contracts
    1. Revocation of Acceptance
    2. Excuses for Nonperformance
    3. Seller's Remedies
    4. Buyer's Remedies

▶ **Negotiable Instruments (UCC Article 3)**
  A. Types of Commercial Paper
  B. Transfer and Negotiation
    1. Primary and Secondary Liability
    2. Endorsements
  C. Holders in Due Course
  D. Checks

▶ **Secured Transactions (UCC Article 9)**
  A. Perfecting a Security Interest
  B. Rights of Perfected Security Interests
  C. Rights of Unperfected Security Interests
  D. Default

▶ **Consumer Law**
  A. Fair Trade Laws
    1. Federal Trade Commission Act
    2. State Unfair Trade Practices Acts
    3. Consumer Warranties: Magnuson-Moss
  B. Consumer Credit Laws
    1. Truth in Lending Act
    2. Fair Credit Reporting Act
    3. Equal Credit Opportunity Act

▶ **Bankruptcy**
  A. Bankruptcy Act
  B. Liquidation Proceedings

▶ **Summary**

When you take the randomized full practice exams in the SMART Online Practice Exams product, you are using the same software you will use when you take the actual exam. Take advantage of your time and learn the features of the software now.

Key Words and Phrases

Define or describe each of the words and phrases listed below.

Implied warranty of fitness for a particular purpose (p. 6.6)

Implied warranty of title (p. 6.6)

FOB (free on board) place of shipment (p. 6.8)

FOB (free on board) place of destination (p. 6.8)

FAS (free alongside) vessel (p. 6.8)

FOB (free on board) vessel (p. 6.8)

CIF (cost-insurance-freight) (p. 6.8)

CAF (cost and freight) (p. 6.8)

COD (collect on delivery) (p. 6.8)

Draft, or check (p. 6.12)

Certificate of deposit (CD) (p. 6.13)

Promissory note (p. 6.13)

Trade acceptance (p. 6.13)

Primary liability (p. 6.14)

Secondary liability (p. 6.14)

Special endorsement (p. 6.14)

Blank, or general endorsement (p. 6.15)

Restrictive, or collection endorsement (p. 6.15)

Qualified endorsement (p. 6.15)

Unqualified endorsement (p. 6.15)

Holder in due course (p. 6.15)

Personal defense (p. 6.15)

Real defense (p. 6.15)

Certified check (p. 6.16)

Cashier's check (p. 6.16)

Security interest (p. 6.17)

Secured transaction (p. 6.17)

Secured party (p. 6.17)

Collateral (p. 6.17)

Pledge (p. 6.17)

Surety (p. 6.17)

Principal (in a surety) (p. 6.17)

Obligee (p. 6.17)

Limited warranty (p. 6.21)

Full warranty (p. 6.22)

Electronic funds transfer (EFT) system (p. 6.24)

Bankruptcy law (p. 6.26)

Chapter 7 (p. 6.26)

Chapter 11 (p. 6.27)

Review Questions

1. What type of transactions does UCC Article 2 govern? (p. 6.3)

2. Under what circumstances will a shipment of nonconforming goods not automatically constitute a breach of contract? (p. 6.4)

3. Name a warranty implied in a sale by a merchant that is not implied in a sale by a nonmerchant? (p. 6.6)

4. What persons, if any, other than the buyer, are covered by the seller's warranties in a transaction for the sale of goods? (p. 6.7)

5. What costs does a seller pay in C.I.F. sales that are not paid in an F.O.B. sale? (p. 6.8)

6. Under the UCC, when does risk of loss not follow title? (p. 6.9)

7. Describe three excuses for nonperformance of a sales contract. (pp. 6.10–6.11)

8. What remedy might be available to a seller who, after delivering the goods to a carrier, discovers that the buyer is insolvent? (p. 6.11)

▶▶

9. Describe the elements of negotiability. (p. 6.12)

10. Why is salability an essential characteristic for negotiable instruments? (p. 6.13)

11. How can the payee of a negotiable instrument negotiate it to another specific person? (p. 6.14)

12. What is the significance of being a holder in due course? (p. 6.15)

13. Identify the characteristics of a holder in due course. (p. 6.15)

14. Why should a financing statement be filed before the security interest attaches to consumer goods? (p. 6.17)

15. Describe two instances in which a perfected security interest is not superior to a later perfected security interest. (p. 6.18)

16. Describe a secured party's options upon a debtor's default. (pp. 6.18–6.19)

17. What, if any, fair trade laws is the insurance business subject to? (pp. 6.19–6.21)

18. Why do manufacturers characterize as "limited" warranties that are essentially full warranties? (p. 6.22)

19. What are the requirements of the Truth in Lending Act? (pp. 6.22–6.23)

20. Identify the practices that violate the Fair Debt Collection Practices Act. (p. 6.24)

21. Under what circumstances might a reporting agency issue a consumer report? (p. 6.25)

22. Distinguish liquidation from reorganization as bankruptcy remedies. (p. 6.26)

23. Who can initiate involuntary bankruptcy proceedings? (p. 6.27)

24. What are the priorities among creditors in a liquidation proceeding? (p. 6.28)

Application Questions

1. Herman, a wholesaler, bought "fully nonmagnetic stainless steel" from a manufacturer who mistakenly shipped stainless steel that was not fully nonmagnetic. Herman sold the steel to a buyer as fully nonmagnetic. The buyer soon found out that the steel was not the type needed and offered to return the steel. He demanded his money back. Herman claimed that it was not his fault and that the buyer should seek recourse from the company that shipped the wrong steel. Is Herman liable to the buyer? If so, why? If not, why not?

2. Wanda purchased certain bulky goods from Selma. The goods were identified and marked with Wanda's name. Wanda was to pick up the goods within a week and make the full payment at that time. During the week, a fire broke out in Selma's place of business. The fire was not a result of Selma's negligence, but the goods were totally destroyed. Answer the following questions relating to these facts:

   a.   Did title to the goods pass to Wanda? If so, when? If not, why not?

   b.   Who bears the risk of loss, or, to put it another way, must Wanda pay for the goods?

3. Identify the following endorsement found on separate instruments, on each of which John Doe is payee, and point out the liabilities, if any, incurred by John Doe:

   a.   Pay to the order of Howard Roe
          /s/ John Doe

   b.   Without recourse
          /s/ John Doe

    c.   Pay to the order of Mary Bright on delivery of 250 barrels
       of oil.

            /s/ John Doe

    d.   For deposit

            /s/ John Doe

4. Ken signed a note as maker that has come into the hands of Joyce,
a good faith purchaser for value and a holder in due course. When
Joyce presented the note for payment, Ken defended on the grounds
that he thought he was signing a receipt for goods from Ellen; that
he had carefully read the receipt to see what it contained; that, after
examining it, Ellen distracted Ken's attention by asking to come to
the window and observe a curious cloud formation; and that, in the
interim, Ellen's friend substituted for the receipt the note in question.
Joyce said to Ken: "The fact that you were taken, if it is a fact, is no
concern of mine. I paid good money for the note that you signed, and
I am entitled to the face amount."

Explain the nature of Ken's defense. On what finding of fact does
its validity depend?

5. A manufacturer sold television sets to George's television shop. The sales were made on credit, and the manufacturer and George signed a security agreement giving the manufacturer a security interest in George's inventory. A financing statement covering this interest was then properly filed. Afterward, George sold one of the sets covered by this agreement to Sidney, a consumer. When George did not pay the manufacturer on time, the manufacturer repossessed the television set from Sidney.

    a.   Did the manufacturer have a perfected security interest in the set?

    b.   Was the manufacturer entitled to possession of the set sold to Sidney when George defaulted? Explain.

Answers to Assignment 6

NOTE: These answers are provided to give students a basic understanding of acceptable types of responses. They often are not the only valid answers and are not intended to provide an exhaustive response to the questions.

Review Questions

1. UCC Article 2 covers the law of sales of goods.

2. A shipment of nonconforming goods does not automatically constitute a breach of contract in the following circumstances:
   - If the seller notifies the buyer that the shipment is only an accommodation to the buyer
   - If a buyer rejects goods as nonconforming before the time for contractual performance has expired. The seller then can notify the buyer of its intention to cure the nonconformity by delivering conforming goods.

3. An implied warranty of merchantability is implied in a sale by a merchant, but not in a sale by a nonmerchant.

4. A seller's warranty extends to any person in the buyer's family or household, or any guest in the buyer's home, who suffers injury resulting from breach of the warranty.

5. A seller pays the cost of insurance and freight charges in a C.I.F. sale, but not in an F.O.B. sale.

6. Under the UCC, risk of loss always follows title except when identified goods are at the seller's residence or place of business and the buyer is to pick them up.

7. Three excuses for nonperformance of a sales contract are the following:
   (1) Loss of identified goods
   (2) Unavailability of agreed-on shipping
   (3) Failure of a presupposed condition

8. If a seller, after delivering the goods to a carrier, discovers that the buyer is insolvent, the seller can withhold delivery of the goods or stop their delivery.

9. A negotiable instrument must have the following elements of negotiability:
   - Be signed by the maker or drawer
   - Contain an unconditional promise to order to pay a certain sum in money
   - Be payable on demand or at a definite time
   - Be payable to order or to bearer

10. Salability is an essential characteristic for negotiable instruments so that the seller does not have to wait for payment once the goods are delivered to the buyer.

11. The payee of a negotiable instrument can negotiate it to another specific person by endorsement.

12. A holder in due course possesses a negotiable instrument but is free of personal defenses.

13. A holder in due course is one who possesses an instrument drawn to his or her order and who has taken the instrument under the following conditions:
    - For value
    - In good faith
    - Without notice that it is overdue or has been dishonored or without notice of any other persons' defenses against or claims to it

14. If the seller delays filing the financing statement until after the delivery of the goods to the buyer, the security interest is unperfected, and another security interest might attach to the property in the meantime.

15. A perfected security interest is not superior to a later perfected security interest in the following two instances:
    (1) A holder in due course takes a negotiable instrument free of any perfected security interest in that instrument.
    (2) An artisan's lien for services or materials with respect to the collateral takes priority over a perfected security interest in that collateral.

16. A secured party's options upon a debtor's default are as follows:
    - Right to sue on the underlying debt
    - Right to foreclose
    - Right to regain possession
    - Right to retain or sell the collateral
    - Right to dispose of the collateral as desired

17. Under the McCarran-Ferguson Act, the federal government generally does not regulate the business of insurance because it is subject to state regulations, and states usually apply their own antitrust laws to insurance. However, if a state does not have antitrust legislation applicable to insurance, federal antitrust laws apply. State laws, including Deceptive Trade Practices Acts, may apply to insurers. Some states have adopted the Model Insurance Fair Trade Practices Act.

18. Manufacturers often characterize warranties that are essentially full warranties as limited to avoid "lemon law" provisions.

19. The Truth in Lending Act requires creditors to disclose finance charges and applies to all persons or organizations that regularly extend credit or make finance charges in connection with installment purchases.

20. The Fair Debt Collection Practices Act prohibits collection practices such as using violent or criminal acts, using profane language, publishing lists of debtors, calling debtors repeatedly or in the middle of the night, threatening legal action with no intent to follow through, and contacting the debtor at work or at any unusual time or place, except with the debtor's consent.

21. A reporting agency can issue a consumer report under the following circumstances:
    - In response to a court order
    - Under written instructions of the subject of the report

- To a person who, it has reason to believe, intends to use the information in connection with a credit transaction, for employment purposes, in connection with insurance underwriting, for determination of eligibility for a business license if the applicant's financial status is relevant, or for a legitimate business need for the information in connection with a business transaction.

22. Liquidation involves selling all the debtor's assets and distributing the proceeds to the creditors. Reorganization means the debtor's affairs are set free of claims of creditors; and partial or full repayment of debts during the reorganization process.

23. Any creditors who believe that a bankrupt person or organization favors other creditors or who continue to dispute the remaining assets of a bankrupt estate can petition the federal bankruptcy court for involuntary bankruptcy.

24. The priorities among creditors in a liquidation proceeding are as follows:
- Administrative expenses of the bankruptcy proceeding
- Unsecured business debts
- A limited amount of wage claims
- Contributions to employee benefit plans
- Claims of unsecured individuals
- Unsecured claims of governmental units

Application Questions

1. Herman is a merchant, and the buyer had the right to rely on his representations as to the fitness of the steel for the purpose Herman intended. The buyer can demand his money from Herman, who can, in turn, obtain reimbursement from the manufacturer of the steel.

2. a. Wanda probably has title to the goods because the assumption is that Selma could pass good title to her, and the goods were marked with Wanda's name. The parties appear to have intended title to pass.

   b. Wanda does not have to pay for the goods. The question of who has title does not affect the risk of loss in this case. Under the UCC, risk of loss follows title except when identified goods are at the seller's place of business or residence and the buyer is to pick them up. If the seller is a merchant, risk of loss does not pass to the buyer until the buyer receives the goods. Selma appears to be a merchant because the question speaks of her business.

3. a. The special endorsement gives John Doe all the rights and liabilities associated with the check.

   b. This qualified endorsement means that John Doe has avoided secondary liability, but the check remains negotiable.

   c. This special endorsement gives Mary Bright the rights and liabilities associated with this check upon delivery of 250 barrels of oil.

   d. This restrictive endorsement limits the check to deposit only by John Doe.

4. Joyce, by being a holder in due course, takes the note free of Ken's personal defenses. Even though Ken may not assert the defense against Joyce, he can sue Ellen and her friend to recover the amount he pays Joyce on the note.

5. a.   The manufacturer filed a financing statement and therefore had a perfected security interest.

    b.   The manufacturer was not entitled to the set sold to Sidney because a person who buys consumer goods from the first buyer for personal purposes buys the goods free of the seller's security interest.

Direct Your Learning

Property Law

Educational Objectives

After learning the content of this assignment, you should be able to:

1. Given a case involving personal property:

   a. Describe what interests in personal property exist.

   b. Describe what interests in intellectual property exist.

   c. Describe the respective rights and duties under a bailment.

   d. Describe the required elements of the transfer of property as a gift.

2. Given a case involving real property:

   a. Describe what interests in real property exist.

   b. Describe the requisites for contracts of sales and deeds.

   c. Determine the nature and creation of any security interests and liens.

   d. Describe what incidental real property rights exist.

   e. Describe what land use restrictions affect the use of real property.

   f. Compare the rights and duties of landlords and tenants.

Study Materials

Required Reading:

▶ The Legal Environment of Insurance
  • Chapter 7

Study Aids:

▶ SMART Online Practice Exams

▶ SMART Study Aids
  • Review Notes and Flash Cards— Assignment 7

Outline

▶ **Personal Property**

   A. Intellectual Property
      1. Copyrights
      2. Patents
   B. Accession
   C. Confusion
   D. Bailments
      1. Bailee's Rights and Duties
      2. Bailor's Rights and Duties
      3. Special Bailments
   E. Gifts

▶ **Real Property**

   A. Real Property Estates
      1. Concurrent Estates
      2. Cooperative Ownership
      3. Condominium Ownership
   B. Real Property Sales
      1. Contracts of Sale
      2. Deeds
   C. Recording and Priorities
   D. Real Estate Security Interests
      1. Mortgages
      2. Trust Deeds
      3. Land Contracts

   E. Mechanics' Liens on Real Property
      1. Priorities for Mechanics' Liens
      2. Foreclosure
      3. Waiver of Lien
   F. Incidental Real Property Rights
      1. Adverse Possession
      2. Rights Under, Above, and on the Land's Surface
      3. Rights to Lateral and Subjacent Support
      4. Water Rights
      5. Ownership of Fixtures
   G. Land Use Restrictions
      1. Incorporeal Interests
      2. Licenses
      3. Government Controls
   H. Landlord and Tenant
      1. Landlords' Rights and Duties
      2. Landlords' Remedies
      3. Tenants' Rights and Duties
      4. Liability of Parties

▶ **Summary**

Set aside a specific, realistic amount of time to study every day.

▶▶

Key Words and Phrases

Define or describe each of the words and phrases listed below.

Property (p. 7.3)

Real property, or realty (p. 7.3)

Personal property (p. 7.3)

Ownership (p. 7.3)

Title (p. 7.3)

Possession (p. 7.3)

Intellectual property rights (p. 7.4)

Copyright (p. 7.4)

Fair use (p. 7.4)

Patent (p. 7.5)

Accession (p. 7.5)

Confusion (p. 7.6)

Bailment (p. 7.6)

Bailor (p. 7.6)

Bailee (p. 7.6)

Lien (p. 7.7)

Possessory lien (p. 7.7)

Common carrier (p. 7.10)

Shipper (p. 7.10)

Factor (p. 7.10)

Gift (p. 7.11)

Donor (p. 7.11)

Donee (p. 7.11)

Fixture (p. 7.11)

Real property estate (p. 7.12)

Interest (p. 7.12)

Fee simple estate (p. 7.12)

Life tenant (p. 7.12)

Tenancy (p. 7.12)

Joint tenancy (p. 7.12)

Tenancy by the entirety (p. 7.13)

Tenancy in common (p. 7.14)

Community property (p. 7.14)

Cooperative ownership (p. 7.14)

Condominium (p. 7.15)

Vendor (p. 7.16)

Vendee (p. 7.16)

Grantor (p. 7.16)

Grantee (p. 7.16)

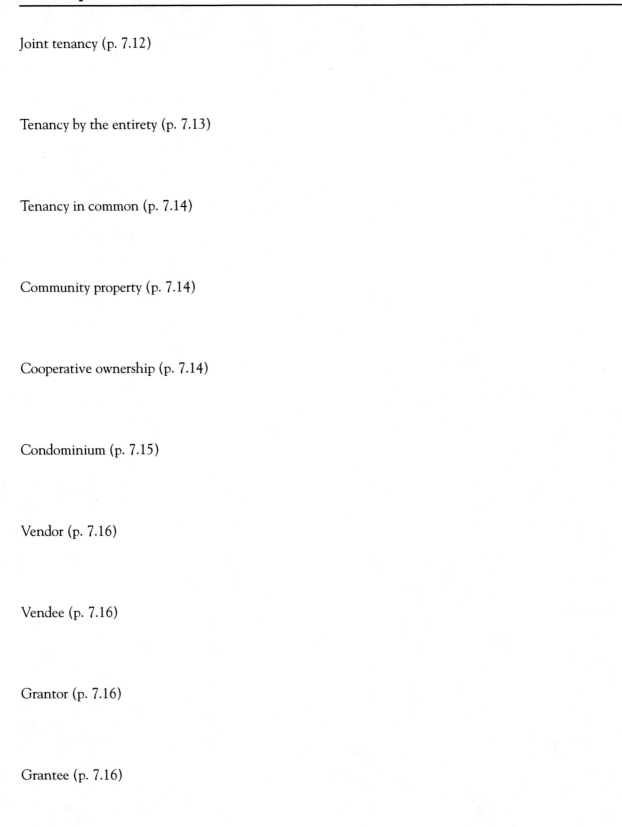

Deed (p. 7.16)

Quit-claim deed (p. 7.16)

General warranty deed (p. 7.17)

Special warranty deed (p. 7.17)

Bargain-and-sale deed (p. 7.17)

Mortgagor (p. 7.18)

Mortgagee (p. 7.18)

Foreclosure (p. 7.19)

Trust deed, or deed of trust, or trust indenture (p. 7.19)

Land contract (p. 7.20)

Mechanic's lien (p. 7.21)

Adverse possession (p. 7.23)

Lateral support (p. 7.23)

Subjacent support (p. 7.24)

Riparian owner (p. 7.24)

Trade fixture (p. 7.25)

Improvements and betterments (p. 7.25)

Incorporeal interest (p. 7.25)

Easement (p. 7.25)

Profits à prendre (p. 7.26)

License (p. 7.26)

Zoning (p. 7.27)

Spot zoning (p. 7.27)

Exclusionary zoning (p. 7.27)

Special exception (p. 7.27)

Variance (p. 7.27)

Hardship variance (p. 7.27)

Use variance (p. 7.27)

Nonconforming use (p. 7.27)

Building codes (p. 7.28)

Eminent domain (p. 7.28)

Condemnation proceeding (p. 7.28)

Tenancy at will (p. 7.28)

Estate for years (p. 7.28)

Periodic tenancy (p. 7.28)

Holdover tenant (p. 7.28)

Tenant at sufferance (p. 7.28)

Security deposit (p. 7.29)

Constructive eviction (p. 7.30)

Distraint (p. 7.30)

Review Questions

1. Distinguish between the rights of ownership and possession. (pp. 7.3–7.4)

2. What problems do the rules of accession and confusion address? (pp. 7.5–7.6)

3. Explain what interests and rights a bailee has in property. (pp. 7.7–7.8)

4. Explain the extent of a bailee's insurable interest. (p. 7.9)

5. Compare the extent of liability of common carriers, hotel-keepers, and warehouse operators. (pp. 7.10–7.11)

6. Describe the three requirements for a gift. (p. 7.11)

7. How are dower and curtesy rights affected by the following:
(p. 7.13)
   a. A will

   b. Divorce

8. Distinguish between joint tenancies and tenancies in common.
(pp. 7.12–7.14)

9. What does a condominium unit owner own? (pp. 7.15–7.16)

▶▶

10. What essential terms must a contract for the sale of real estate contain? (p. 7.16)

11. Would a buyer prefer a general warranty deed or a special warranty deed? (p. 7.17)

12. What are the requirements of a deed? (p. 7.17)

13. Why is the recording of a deed important? (pp. 7.17–7.18)

14. What rights does a mortgagee have against the following: (pp. 7.18–7.19)

    a.   The owner

b. A subsequent purchaser

15. In what situations are the following most suitable? (pp. 7.19–7.20)
    a. Trust deeds

    b. Land contracts

16. What are the requirements for one to obtain title by adverse possession of the lands of another? (pp. 7.22–7.23)

17. Explain the tests for whether particular property is a fixture. (pp. 7.24–7.25)

18. How can easements be created? (p. 7.25)

19. Give some examples of profits *à prendre*. (p. 7.26)

20. What matters do zoning laws and building codes, respectively, typically control? (p. 7.27)

21. What is the landlord's primary duty? (p. 7.29)

22. What are a landlord's remedies against a tenant? (pp. 7.29–7.30)

23. What are a tenant's primary rights and duties? (p. 7.30)

24. Who is liable for injuries to third parties on rented or leased property? (pp. 7.30–7.31)

Application Questions

1. Felicia, the driver of a truck for Yale Company, a common carrier, parked her truck at a roadside diner to have lunch. While Felicia was in the diner, thieves broke into the locked truck and stole the contents.

   a. Based on general bailment principles, what, if anything, is Yale Company's liability to the owners of the contents? Explain.

   b. Would your answer be different if the contract of carriage specifically provided that the carrier was not to be liable for any damage or loss to goods not caused by its negligence? Why or why not?

2. During his marriage, Harry purchased a home in his name only. If Harry desires to sell the home, should his wife's signature be on the deed (a) in a common-law state or (b) in a community property state?

3. Doug borrowed $15,000 from his parents to help him purchase a home. Doug gave a mortgage document to the parents that they chose not to record to evade certain taxes. Doug then placed another mortgage on the property for $150,000 with Bank Y, which recorded the mortgage. Jerry, a creditor of Doug, later obtained a judgment for $5,000 against Doug. In the event of judicial sale, what are the priorities of the parents' claim, Bank Y's claim, and Jerry's claim? Why?

4. Jessica's father died thirty years ago, and her mother had lived on the family farm until her mother's recent death. Jessica is the sole beneficiary under her mother's will and is carrying out the terms of the will, which directs that the title to the farm should pass to Jessica.

   a. Jessica received a letter from a roofer demanding that she pay her mother's debt for recently installing new roofing on the barn. Describe the following with regard to the roofer.

      (1) The legal right available to obtain payment for the work on the barn

(2) The roofer's remedy to enforce this legal right if Jessica refuses to pay

b.   Matt has lived in an out-building on the farm for twenty years. After Jessica's mother's death, Matt moves into the main farmhouse. Jessica had received a letter from Matt's attorney, claiming that Matt has legal ownership of the farm. Citing the requisites of adverse possession, explain whether Matt can prove that he is the legal owner of the farm, and why or why not.

5. In 2005, Bryan sold some land to Oliver. The deed provided that the land was not to be used for either of the following:

a.   Maintaining any automobile garage on the premises
b.   Any building for the manufacture of glue, gun powder, or fertilizers

Are the restrictions binding on Oliver? Explain.

Answers to Assignment 7 Questions

NOTE: These answers are provided to give students a basic understanding of acceptable types of responses. They often are not the only valid answers and are not intended to provide an exhaustive response to the questions.

Review Questions

1. Ownership is a relationship between the owner and the rest of society that includes rights of the owner specific to the property. Possession is the exercise of custody or control over property, and is not, in itself, ownership.

2. Accession addresses the problem of one person's adding value to another person's personal property without the owner's consent. Confusion addresses the problem of whether the mingling of goods belonging to different owners was accidental or intentional.

3. A bailee has possession only and has the right to hold the property (possessory lien) as security for payment.

4. The bailee has an insurable interest in goods because of the bailee's legal duty to care for the goods and to return them to the bailor. A bailee must hold insurance proceeds paid for the bailed property's damage in trust for the bailor. However, in the absence of a statute or specific contract requirement, a bailee has no duty to obtain insurance on the bailed goods.

5. A common carrier is liable from the time it receives the goods until their delivery to a freight terminal or until the recipient has had reasonable time to inspect and remove the goods from the carrier or terminal. Hotelkeepers are liable only for failure to exercise reasonable care in protecting guests' property, a liability that can be limited by providing safes for storing guests' valuables. Warehouse operators do not insure stored goods and can limit liability in the warehouse receipt issued for goods received.

6. The following are the three requirements for a gift:
    (1) Donative intent
    (2) Delivery
    (3) Acceptance

7. Even though a spouse's will gives the surviving spouse less than the rightful dower or curtesy portion, the surviving spouse can elect to receive the dower portion. Divorce, however, bars dower and curtesy rights.

8. In joint tenancies, the estate goes entirely to the other joint tenant in the event of one joint tenant's death; joint tenants hold equal shares; all conditions apply equally to all joint tenants; and the same deed must name all joint tenants as owners. Tenancies in common, however, involve no survivorship, allow parties to own unequal shares, and do not require parties to derive their interests in the same deed from the same grantor.

9. A condominium unit owner owns an individual unit, or separate, defined area, as well as an undivided interest in common or public areas that serve all individal units.

10. A contract of sale for real estate requires the following three essential elements:

   (1) The contract must be in writing.

   (2) The contract must list the essential terms of the contract, such as a description of the premises to be sold and the price of the premises.

   (3) The contract must list the nonessential terms of the contract, such as the time of closing.

11. A buyer would prefer a general warranty deed because a special warranty deed does not protect the buyer against earlier defects in the property.

12. The requirements of a deed are as follows:

   • The deed must be in writing.

   • The grantor must be legally competent and must sign the deed.

   • The deed must name the grantee.

   • The deed must state the consideration.

   • The deed must contain words that specifically state that a transfer of the property is occurring.

   • The deed must contain a description of the property conveyed.

   • The deed must be dated.

   • The deed may contain a paragraph relating to the transferor of the property, date of transfer, and location of the recorded copy of the deed.

   • Some states require the grantor's signature under seal.

   • Some states require witnesses to the grantor's signature.

   • The deed must be delivered.

   • Most states require an acknowledgement, usually by the notary public.

13. Without the recording of a deed, no public notice exists that the transfer of real property has occurred.

14. a. A mortgagee has the right to foreclose against the owner if the loan is not paid when due, and to obtain deficiency judgments against owners for the remainder of the loan after the property is sold.

   b. A mortgagee may also collect deficient payments from a subsequent purchaser after foreclosure.

15. a. Trust deeds are most suitable when large loans are involved.

   b. Buyers frequently use land contracts when they have poor or inadequate credit ratings or do not have enough money for down payments.

16. The requirements for obtaining title by adverse possession of another person's land are as follows:

   • The adverse party must have exclusive possession of the property and occupy it in the usual way.

   • Possession must be open and obvious.

   • Possession must be adverse, or hostile, and without the owner's permission.

   • Possession must be continuous for a statutory period, usually a lengthy period, such as twenty years or more.

17. Three tests determine whether property is a fixture:

   (1) The article cannot be removed without substantial injury to the realty.

   (2) The article is specially constructed or fitted for use in a building, or the article is installed in the building to enable people to use the building.

   (3) The party who attached an item intended it to become part of the land or building.

18. Easements can be created by express words, by implication, or by prescription (adverse possession).

19. The rights to mine coal, remove sand and gravel, or cut down trees are profits à *prendre*.

20. Zoning laws regulate building construction and occupancy and land use according to a comprehensive plan. Building codes regulate technical construction details, such as electrical wiring and heating.

21. The landlord's primary duty is to deliver possession of the premises to the tenant on the lease's inception date.

22. A landlord's remedies against a tenant are the right to evict a tenant or apply to a court for help in the event of a tenant's breach of lease. The landlord can also seize a tenant's property and hold it for unpaid rent (distraint) or may impose a nonpossessory lien on a tenant's property for rent due.

23. A tenant's primary right is the right to occupy the premises. A tenant's primary duty is to leave the premises in the same condition they were in at the lease inception, except for reasonable wear and tear.

24. Landlords are liable for injuries to third parties if the injury is the result of a landlord's negligent acts or latent defects on the premises.

Application Questions

1. a. This is a bailment for mutual benefit. The Yale Company, through Felicia as its employee, was a bailee of the goods and had the duty to exercise reasonable care under the circumstances with regard to the goods. If a bailee exercises such care, any loss or damage to the bailed property falls upon the bailors, who hold title to the goods.

   b. A contract might limit a common carrier's liability to a shipper, although the carrier might not escape liability for negligence completely. There was no negligence indicated in this case, so the contractual provision for release of liability would be effective.

2. a. If applicable state law allows a spouse to own property individually, as it apparently does in this case, then Harry can sell the property with his signature only.

   b. In a community property state, the wife's signature would be required for transfer of the property. The facts imply that the couple acquired this property during marriage, and the married couple jointly owns all property so acquired.

3. The following claims are listed in order of descending priority:

   Bank Y—Bank Y recorded its mortgage and therefore has first priority. An unrecorded mortgage (the parents' loan) is not valid against good-faith purchasers, a subsequent mortgagee without knowledge, or creditors with liens on the property. Bank Y is a subsequent mortgagee without knowledge.

   Jerry's claim—Jerry won a lawsuit, which is effectively a lien on Doug's property. His claim takes priority over the parents' unrecorded mortgage.

Doug's parents' claim—The parents failed to give notice to the world that they even had a claim, and parties who acquire subsequent interests in the property without such notice should not suffer from the parents' inaction.

4. a. (1) The roofer can obtain a mechanic's lien on the property. A mechanic's lien can be claimed by any person who contributes labor and material to the improvement of real property. The roofer should file notice of the mechanic's lien, and the applicable state law will determine the priorities of the roofer's lien in relationship to any other liens.

    (2) The roofer can foreclose, forcing a court sale of the property and receiving a share of the proceeds equal to the amount owed.

    b. Even though Matt lived on the land for twenty years, he did not have exclusive possession of the farm for most of that time because Jessica's mother lived in the farmhouse until her recent death. Matt's adverse possession claim to the farm would fail on this basis.

5. Bryan can place restrictions on the use of the property as long as those restrictions are not discriminatory or otherwise unenforceable, such as requiring an illegal use. However, state law may limit the restrictions to a period of years, and changed conditions, such as economic conditions in the area, can make the restrictions unenforceable. For example, if the land had been scenic and rural, but then developed into a strip of businesses, including other automobile garages and the like, the restriction might end. Another example would be that employment becomes depressed in the area, and making glue, gunpowder, or fertilizers becomes the most effective economic relief. Such developments could end the restrictions.

Direct Your Learning

Tort Law—Negligence

Educational Objectives

After learning the content of this assignment, you should be able to:

1. Given a case, explain which classification of tort law and state law applies.

2. Given a case, determine whether the elements of negligence are present.

    a. Describe the elements required to prove negligence.

    b. Describe the various proofs of negligence and of imputed negligence.

3. Given a case, explain whether any of the following defenses would affect a plaintiff's right to recovery:

    a. Contributory negligence

    b. Comparative negligence

    c. Last clear chance

    d. Assumption of risk

    e. Release of liability

    f. Immunity

4. Explain how a person can assume vicarious liability by hiring independent contractors.

5. Explain how the following agreements affect contractual liability:

    a. Liquidated damages agreement

    b. Hold-harmless agreement

    c. Exculpatory agreement

6. Given a case, evaluate the liability of landowners or occupiers for negligence relating to natural or artificial conditions.

Study Materials

Required Reading:
▶ The Legal Environment of Insurance
 • Chapter 8

Study Aids:
▶ SMART Online Practice Exams
▶ SMART Study Aids
 • Review Notes and Flash Cards— Assignment 8

Outline

▶ **Definition and Classification of Torts**

▶ **Applicable Law**

▶ **Negligence**

    A. Elements of Negligence

        1. Legal Duty

        2. Breach of Duty

        3. Proximate Cause

        4. Actual Injury or Damage

    B. Proof of Negligence

        1. Negligence per Se

        2. Res Ipsa Loquitur

    C. Imputed Negligence

        1. Imputed Contributory Negligence

        2. Vicarious Liability

    D. Defenses to Negligence Actions

        1. Contributory Negligence

        2. Comparative Negligence

        3. Last Clear Chance

        4. Assumption of Risk

        5. Release of Liability

        6. Immunity From Liability

        7. Independent Contractors

        8. Contractual Liability

▶ **Liability of Landowners and Occupiers for Negligence**

    A. Natural Conditions

    B. Artificial Conditions

        1. Hidden Dangers

        2. Attractive Nuisance

        3. Sidewalks and Streets

    C. Licenses

        1. Licensee

        2. Invitee

    D. Hotel Operators

    E. Landlords

▶ **Summary**

Plan to take one week to complete each assignment in your course.

Key Words and Phrases

Define or describe each of the words and phrases listed below.

Tort (p. 8.3)

Intentional tort (p. 8.4)

Tortfeasor (p. 8.4)

Forum (p. 8.5)

Situs (p. 8.5)

Rule of significant contacts (p. 8.5)

Negligence (p. 8.6)

Legal duty (p. 8.6)

Trespasser (p. 8.7)

Licensee (p. 8.8)

Invitee (p. 8.8)

Reasonable person test (p. 8.8)

Reckless misconduct (p. 8.10)

Proximate cause (p. 8.11)

"But for" rule (p. 8.12)

Substantial factor rule (p. 8.12)

Foreseeability rule (p. 8.12)

Intervening act (p. 8.13)

Concurrent causation (p. 8.13)

Negligence per se (p. 8.13)

Res ipsa loquitur (p. 8.14)

Exclusive control (p. 8.14)

Imputed negligence (p. 8.15)

Imputed contributory negligence (p. 8.15)

Vicarious liability (p. 8.15)

Negligent entrustment (p. 8.16)

Dangerous instrumentality doctrine (p. 8.16)

Negligent supervision (p. 8.16)

Contributory negligence (p. 8.17)

Comparative negligence (p. 8.17)

Pure comparative negligence rule (p. 8.18)

50 percent comparative negligence rule (p. 8.18)

49 percent comparative negligence rule (p. 8.18)

Slight versus gross rule (p. 8.18)

Last clear chance doctrine (p. 8.19)

Assumption-of-risk defense (p. 8.20)

Sovereign, or governmental, immunity (p. 8.21)

Proprietary function (p. 8.22)

Governmental function (p. 8.22)

Objective reasonableness standard (p. 8.22)

Administrative, or discretionary, act (p. 8.23)

Ministerial act (p. 8.23)

Quasi-governmental theory (p. 8.23)

Trust fund theory (p. 8.23)

Interspousal immunity (p. 8.23)

Parent-child immunity (p. 8.24)

Hold-harmless, or indemnity, agreement (p. 8.25)

Nuisance (p. 8.27)

Attractive nuisance doctrine (p. 8.28)

Express license (p. 8.29)

Implied license (p. 8.29)

Public invitee (p. 8.29)

Business invitee (p. 8.29)

Review Questions

1. Explain why the location and interest analysis rules (*lex loci* and rule of significant contacts) might result in the application of different laws to a given test case. (pp. 8.5–8.6)

2. What are the four elements of negligence? (p. 8.6)

3. Describe the ways in which a legal duty can arise. (pp. 8.6–8.8)

4. Explain the standard of care applicable to the following persons:
   (pp. 8.8–8.9)

   a. People with disabilities

   b. Professionals

5. What important legal consequences depend on the distinction
   between negligence and reckless misconduct? (pp. 8.10–8.11)

6. Explain the rules for determining proximate cause.
   (pp. 8.12–8.13)

7. Explain under what circumstances the doctrine of *res ipsa loquitur*
   applies. (p. 8.14)

8. Describe the situations in which imputed negligence can arise. (p. 8.15)

9. Explain whether, when a mother gives the keys of her automobile to her fifteen-year-old son, either or both of the following apply: negligent entrustment or negligent supervision. (p. 8.16)

10. What is the effect, at common law, of a finding of contributory negligence on the plaintiff's part? (p. 8.17)

11. What criticism has been made of pure comparative negligence rules? (p. 8.18)

12. What is the purpose of the doctrine of last clear chance? (pp. 8.19–8.20)

13. What two circumstances establish the assumption of risk defense? (p. 8.20)

14. What types of activities performed by a government are not covered by the doctrine of sovereign immunity? (p. 8.21)

15. What is the current status of the defense of inter-spousal immunity? (pp. 8.23–8.24)

16. Under what circumstances might a person be liable for the torts of an independent contractor? (pp. 8.24–8.25)

17. Under what circumstances is an exculpatory agreement valid? (p. 8.26)

18. Explain what constitutes an attractive nuisance. (p. 8.28)

19. Distinguish between the duties a landowner owes to a licensee and those owed to an invitee. (p. 8.29)

Application Questions

1. Mitch gives the keys to his car to his son, Steve, who is sixteen years old and who does not have a driver's license. Mitch knows Steve is a poor driver. Steve drives negligently and causes an accident, in which Peter is injured. Discuss:

   a. Steve's potential liability to Peter

   b. Mitch's potential liability to Peter

2. Joanna, the owner of a canoe rental service, rented a canoe to Alan, knowing that Alan was intoxicated and unfit to use it. Alan upset the canoe and began screaming for help. Joanna got into the canoe and went out to assist Alan. The bow of her canoe hit Alan in the head. Alan drowned. Discuss Joanna's liability, including:

   a. Joanna's duty to Alan

   b. Joanna's breach of duty

   c. Joanna's potential liability to Alan's estate and family

3. Tim and Mary collide at an intersection. Tim sues Mary for damages, alleging that Mary was negligent. Mary files a counterclaim alleging that Tim was negligent and, further, that Tim saw Mary and could have avoided the accident. The jury found Tim was 49 percent negligent, and Mary was 51 percent negligent. What would the result be if:

   a. The action was in a state that applies the contributory negligence defense?

b.   The state had a pure comparative negligence rule?

c.   The state had a 49 percent comparative negligence rule?

d.   The jury also found that Tim had a chance to avoid the accident but did not do so?

4. Jane, while soldering a pipe joint in the process of installing plumbing in a new house, negligently set fire to the structure. The owner sues Jane and also sues Brad, the plumbing contractor for whom Jane works as an employee, and Lyle, the general contractor.

a.   On what theory might Brad be liable for Jane's acts?

b.   On what theory might Lyle be liable for Jane's acts?

c. Is Jane also liable under these facts?

d. What potential defenses might Brad and Lyle have to such action?

5. Prospect invited Producer to his home to discuss his insurance program. Producer arrived late one afternoon. When Producer left, it was dark, and Prospect's thirty-foot walk was lit dimly by a forty-watt yellow porch-light bulb. Producer failed to see eight concrete steps outside the gate going down to the street, fell down the steps, and broke her arm. She sued Prospect for damages.

a. What was Producer's status on Prospect's property?

b. What duties, if any, did Prospect owe to Producer?

c. Was Prospect liable to Producer in this situation? Justify your answer.

Answers to Assignment 8 Questions

NOTE: These answers are provided to give students a basic understanding of acceptable types of responses. They often are not the only valid answers and are not intended to provide an exhaustive response to the questions.

Review Questions

1. This rule often applies in cases involving parties from different states with conflicting laws. A court using *lex loci* would apply the law of the state in which the wrong occurred. Depending on the circumstances, a court using interest analysis will select the law of the state having a greater interest in protecting its citizens by applying its law to each specific case.

2. The four elements of negligence are as follows:
   (1) The defendant's legal duty of care to the plaintiff
   (2) The defendant's breach of the duty
   (3) Proximate cause
   (4) Plaintiff's actual loss or damage

3. Legal duty arises when the parties are in such a relationship that the law imposes on one party a responsibility for the exercise of care toward the other.

4. a. The standard of care applicable to persons with disabilities is based on how a reasonable person with a disability would act under the circumstances.
   b. The standard of care applicable to professionals is based on the skill and knowledge of average members of that profession in the same community when applied with reasonable care.

5. If a tort involves reckless misconduct, the defense that the plaintiff was also negligent might not be sufficient. Additionally, courts can award punitive damages; they can impose liability on a landowner for injury to a trespasser. Finally, automobile guest statutes do not permit recovery for ordinary negligence, but do for reckless misconduct.

6. The rules for determining proximate cause are as follows:
   - "But for" rule
   - Substantial factor rule
   - Proof of defendant's responsibility
   - Foreseeability rule

7. The doctrine of *res ipsa loquitur* applies in these circumstances:
   - When the probability exists that the defendant was negligent
   - When the defendant, as the party who had exclusive control of, and who therefore had superior knowledge of, the causative circumstances, has the duty to explain the event in question.

8. Imputed negligence can arise in situations in which passengers injured in auto accidents were assumed to be aware of the driver's skills, or lack of them, and were therefore considered negligent and unable to recover damages. Similarly, in a lawsuit in which one spouse sues another party for personal injury, and the other spouse is found to have contributed to the first spouse's injury through negligence, that negligence is imputed to the injured spouse, who is then barred from recovery of damages.

9. When a mother gives the keys of her automobile to her fifteen-year-old son, there are grounds for both negligent entrustment and negligent supervision if the son injures a person or damages property while driving the automobile.

10. At common law, a finding of contributory negligence on the plaintiff's part bars the plaintiff from recovering in a lawsuit.

11. The pure comparative negligence rule is criticized because it does not base recovery on apportionment of fault, but on the relative amount of loss; thus a party whose negligence was a major factor in the incident can recover damages from a party who was less at fault.

12. The purpose of the doctrine of last clear chance is to alleviate the harsh results of contributory negligence.

13. The two circumstances that establish assumption of risk are proof that the plaintiff had full knowledge of the risk and that, having an opportunity to elect to avoid it, voluntarily chose to incur it.

14. Government activities not covered by sovereign immunity are those that can be performed by entities other than governments.

15. All states have abolished inter-spousal immunity in whole or in part.

16. A person can be liable for an independent contractor's torts if the person negligently employs that contractor, delegates performance of nondelegable duties to the contractor, or employs an independent contractor to do work that is inherently dangerous to others.

17. An exculpatory agreement is valid under any of the following conditions:
    *   The exculpatory clause is not adverse to a public interest and not against public policy.
    *   The party excused from liability is not under a duty to perform.
    *   The contract does not grow out of the parties' unequal bargaining power and is not otherwise unconscionable.

18. An attractive nuisance is something artificial on the land that is certain to attract children.

19. A landowner owes an adult licensee the affirmative duty to refrain from willfully or wantonly injuring the person or acting in a way that would increase that person's peril. For invitees, the landowner owes a duty to exercise reasonable care to keep the premises reasonably safe and to warn of concealed dangerous conditions.

Applications Questions

1. a. Steve is liable for his negligence. Minors over fourteen are presumed capable of negligence, but many states apply the standard that minors should be held to the same standard of care as other minors similar in age, experience, capacity, and development and in similar circumstances. Further, a minor who engages in an activity usually undertaken only by adults, such as driving an auto, is held to the same standard of care as an adult.

    b. Mitch is liable for negligent entrustment. He negligently allowed Steve to use an auto, an instrument that could cause harm. He knew Steve did not have a license and, in fact, was a poor driver. The accident was the natural result of such negligent entrustment.

2. a. Joanna may be liable to Alan because she did not use due care in renting the canoe to an intoxicated customer.

   b. Joanna breached her duty when she rented the canoe to Alan.

   c. Joanna is potentially liable for negligence and negligent entrustment for the following reasons:

   • She was negligent in that she had a legal duty, she failed to conform to the appropriate standard of care, there was a causal connection between Joanna's negligence and Alan's death, and Alan suffered a loss of life.

   • She is liable for negligent entrustment in that she carelessly allowed Alan to operate the canoe, and Alan's incompetence was the proximate cause of his death.

   • Joanna's rental of a canoe to an intoxicated person might be considered reckless misconduct for which Joanna may be subject to punitive damages.

3. a. In a contributory negligence state, Tim would collect nothing because he contributed toward his own injury.

   b. Under a pure comparative negligence rule, Tim would recover damages diminished by his proportion of the total negligence. Tim would recover 51 percent of the damages he claims in this case.

   c. Under a 49 percent comparative negligence rule, Tim can recover reduced damages so long as his negligence is less than, or not as great as, the other party's. Here Tim's negligence was adjudged at 49 percent of the total negligence, so he would recover damages reduced by his proportion (49 percent) of the total negligence.

   d. Under the doctrine of last clear chance, Tim could lose the case. Under this doctrine, the one who has the last clear chance to avoid an injury and fails to do so is solely responsible for its happening.

4. a. Brad is Jane's employer and could be vicariously liable for her work unless a court determines that Jane actually is an independent contractor.

   b. Generally, the employer (Lyle) of an independent contractor (Brad) is not liable for the independent contractor's torts, with some exceptions. One exception is that for inherently dangerous work. Thus, a question in this case is whether soldering is inherently dangerous. A court would decide that question based on prior cases (precedents) in state courts defining inherently dangerous work.

   c. If Jane is an independent contractor, she could be liable.

   d. Brad might say that he had no control over Jane's work and that she is, in reality, a professional and an independent contractor responsible for her own negligence. Lyle might argue that he was not negligent in choosing Brad, a plumbing contractor, and that only Brad is responsible for the torts of his own employee, Jane.

5. (A student should note that, in reality, contracts among all these parties might determine liability. Hold-harmless and exculpatory clauses could govern the relative liabilities in this case.)

   a. Producer is a licensee. She was neither a public nor a business invitee, which are special types of licensees. Even though she was on the property to conduct business, she does not fall into either of these invitee categories.

   b. Prospect owed Producer the duty to refrain from willful and wanton injury and to warn her of hidden defects. Otherwise, Producer took the property in the condition in which it existed.

   c. Prospect was not liable in this situation because the facts reveal no violation of duty.

Direct Your Learning

Tort Law—Intentional Torts

Study Materials

Required Reading:
▶ The Legal Environment of Insurance
  • Chapter 9

Study Aids:
▶ SMART Online Practice Exams
▶ SMART Study Aids
  • Review Notes and Flash Cards—Assignment 9

Educational Objectives

After learning the content of this assignment, you should be able to:

1. Describe each of the following physical torts, the circumstances under which it can occur, and any defenses to it:

   a. Battery

   b. Assault

   c. False imprisonment and false arrest

   d. Intentional infliction of emotional distress

2. Describe each of the following types of defamation, the circumstances under which it can occur, and any defenses to it:

   a. Libel

   b. Slander

3. Describe each of the following types of intentional torts, the circumstances under which it can occur, and any defenses to it:

   a. Invasion of the right of privacy

   b. Fraud

   c. Bad faith, or outrage

   d. Interference with the relationships between others

   e. Misuse of legal process

4. Describe each of the following types of intentional torts, the circumstances under which it can occur, and any defenses to it:

   a. Trespass

   b. Conversion

   c. Nuisance

Outline

▶ **Intentional Physical Torts Against Persons**

   A. Battery

   B. Assault

   C. False Imprisonment and False Arrest

   D. Infliction of Emotional Distress

▶ **Defamation**

   A. Slander

   B. Libel

      1. Libel per Se

      2. News Media

      3. Defenses

      4. Commercial Speech

▶ **Invasion of Right of Privacy**

   A. Intrusion on Solitude or Seclusion

   B. Physical Invasion

   C. Torts Involving Use or Disclosure of Information

   D. Defenses

▶ **Fraud**

▶ **Bad Faith, or Outrage**

   A. Damages

   B. Insurance Cases

   C. Defenses

▶ **Interference With Relationships Between Others**

   A. Injurious Falsehood

   B. Malicious Interference With Prospective Economic Advantage

      1. Common-Law Principles

      2. Defense

   C. Unfair Competition

   D. Interference With Employment

      1. Procuring Employee's Discharge

      2. Preventing Employment

      3. Violating Implied Contract Provisions

      4. Defenses

   E. Interference With Copyright, Patent, or Trademark

   F. Interference With Right to Use One's Own Name in Business

   G. Interference With Family Relationships

▶ **Misuse of Legal Process**

   A. Malicious Prosecution

      1. Defenses

   B. Malicious Abuse of Process

▶ **Intentional Torts Against Property**

   A. Trespass

      1. Trespass to Real Property

      2. Trespass to Personal Property

   B. Conversion

      1. Acquisition of Possession

      2. Unauthorized Transfer of Chattel (Personal Property)

      3. Unreasonable Withholding of Chattel

      4. Damaging, Altering, or Misusing Chattel

      5. Defenses

▶ **Nuisance**

▶ **Summary**

Try to establish a study area away from any distractions, to be used only for studying.

Key Words and Phrases

Define or describe each of the words and phrases listed below.

Battery (p. 9.3)

Assault (p. 9.4)

False imprisonment (p. 9.5)

False arrest (p. 9.5)

Intentional infliction of emotional distress (p. 9.7)

Negligent infliction of emotional distress (p. 9.7)

Defamation (p. 9.8)

Slander (p. 9.8)

Publication (p. 9.8)

Slander per se (p. 9.9)

Libel (p. 9.9)

Libel per se (p. 9.10)

Product disparagement, or trade libel (p. 9.14)

Invasion of the right of privacy, or invasion of privacy (p. 9.14)

Bad faith, or outrage (p. 9.18)

Injurious falsehood (p. 9.20)

Malicious interference with prospective economic advantage (p. 9.21)

Malice (p. 9.22)

Unfair competition (p. 9.22)

Interference with employment (p. 9.22)

Wrongful-life action (p. 9.26)

Wrongful-pregnancy action, or wrongful-conception action (p. 9.26)

Malicious prosecution (p. 9.26)

Probable cause (p. 9.27)

Malicious abuse of process (p. 9.28)

Conversion (p. 9.30)

Chattel (p. 9.30)

Private nuisance (p. 9.32)

Intentional nuisance (p. 9.32)

Nuisance per se (p. 9.32)

Public nuisance (p. 9.32)

Review Questions

1. Is it possible to have a battery without an assault, or vise versa? Give examples. (pp. 9.3–9.5)

2. What are the defenses to assault and battery? (p. 9.5)

3. Under what circumstances can a private citizen make a valid arrest with respect to (a) a felony and (b) a misdemeanor? (pp. 9.6–9.7)

4. Can a plaintiff who suffers no physical injury succeed in a claim for infliction of emotional distress? (p. 9.7)

5. What is the effect of a finding of slander per se or libel per se? (p. 9.9)

6. What protection did *Sullivan v. New York Times* give the media? (p. 9.10)

7. List the defenses to defamation (libel or slander). (p. 9.11)

8. Describe the (a) six types of invasion of privacy and (b) seven defenses for such claims. (pp. 9.14–9.17)

9. What elements must a plaintiff prove to establish fraud? (pp. 9.17–9.18)

10. Explain under what circumstances an insured can sue an insurer for bad faith. (p. 9.19)

11. Under what circumstances does interference with employment arise? (pp. 9.22–9.23)

12. What rights do spouses have against third parties? (pp. 9.25–9.26)

13. Distinguish between malicious prosecution and malicious abuse of process. (pp. 9.26–9.28)

14. How do trespass to real property and trespass to personal property differ? (pp. 9.29–9.30)

15. Describe four different circumstances that can constitute conversions. (pp. 9.30–9.31)

16. Is Jack throwing rubbish in his neighbor's yard a nuisance? (pp. 9.32–9.33)

17. If Joe plays his music very loudly and keeps his neighbors awake, is Joe's act a nuisance? (pp. 9.32–9.33)

Application Questions

1. A child was kidnapped and later returned for a ransom. Aside from criminal charges, enumerate the grounds for a tort lawsuit the parents can file against the kidnappers.

2. For each of the following, indicate whether a tort has occurred and identify the tort, if committed, justifying your choice.

   a.   A surgeon performs an unauthorized operation on an unconscious patient.

   b.   A store manager prevents a suspected shoplifter from leaving the premises for three hours.

   c.   A person steals a car and sells it.

   d.   A newspaper prints a story that says a well-known politician is suspected of bribery.

   e.   Jeff files a complaint to have Scott declared incompetent to acquire control over Scott's assets.

3. The insurance agency where Jerry worked recently laid him off. He has had great difficulty finding a job. One problem he just discovered is that his former supervisor has not been giving him a good recommendation and has been saying he was not effective in his former position. She also has accused him of alcohol abuse.

   a.   Does Jerry have grounds to sue for defamation?

   b.   Does Jerry have grounds to sue for interference with employment?

   c.   Does Jerry have grounds to sue for invasion of the right of privacy?

4. Rob had a disfiguring scar on his face, and a plastic surgeon removed it. Without Rob's permission, the surgeon used photos of Rob's face before and after the surgery to promote his services to prospective patients. On what grounds can Rob sue the surgeon?

5. Mikey and Jimmy, two seven-year-olds, were trading comic books. Jimmy's father told Jimmy to try to get Mikey's "Captain Flyer" because Jimmy's father knew the comic book to be of great value. Neither Mikey nor Mikey's parents knew the true value of the comic book, so Mikey traded it for Jimmy's "Gray Lynx." Mikey's mother has discovered the true value of the comic book. Can she sue to get it back? On what grounds, if any?

Answers to Assignment 9 Questions

NOTE: These answers are provided to give students a basic understanding of acceptable types of responses. They often are not the only valid answers and are not intended to provide an exhaustive response to the questions.

Review Questions

1. A battery can occur without an assault, and vise versa. Touching someone else's clothing can be battery, but not assault, if no threatening gesture occurs to cause apprehension in the victim. Swinging a fist close to someone's face without touching that person is assault without battery.

2. The defenses to assault and battery are that the plaintiff consented to the touching (for battery), that the defendant acted in self-defense or in defense of others, or that the defendant was using physical discipline with reasonable force or in good faith.

3. Citizens can make arrests for felonies committed out of their presence, provided they have reasonable grounds to believe that those arrested committed the felonies. Private citizens can make arrests for misdemeanors only when they constitute breaches of the peace.

4. In many courts, a plaintiff who suffers no physical injury can succeed in a claim for infliction of emotional distress if a physical impact (manifestation) of the emotional distress results.

5. The effect of a finding of slander per se or libel per se is that the plaintiff is not required to prove injury or damage.

6. The protection that *Sullivan v. New York Times* gave the media is that public officials suing for defamation must prove that the defendant's statement was false and that the defendant made it with knowledge of its falsity or with reckless disregard for its truth or falsity.

7. The following are defenses to defamation (libel or slander):
   - Truth
   - Retraction
   - Absolute privilege
   - Conditional or qualified privilege

8. a. The following are the six types of invasion of privacy:
      (1) Intrusion on solitude or seclusion
      (2) Physical invasion
      (3) Public disclosure of private facts
      (4) Publicity placing plaintiff in a false light
      (5) Unauthorized release of confidential information
      (6) Appropriation of plaintiff's name or likeness

   b. The following are the seven defenses for invasion of privacy claims:
      (1) The plaintiff previously published the information.
      (2) The plaintiff consented to publication.
      (3) The plaintiff is a public figure, or the information is public knowledge.

(4) The information was part of a news event.

(5) The publication would not offend an individual of ordinary sensibility.

(6) Matters were disclosed in judicial proceedings.

(7) The information is of public interest.

9. A plaintiff must prove the following six elements to establish fraud:

(1) False representation

(2) Material fact

(3) Knowingly made

(4) Intent to influence or deceive

(5) Reasonable reliance

(6) Detriment

10. An insured can sue an insurer for bad faith when the insurer has failed in its implied duty to act fairly and in good faith in discharging its duties under an insurance contract.

11. Interference with employment arises when a third party has procured the employee's discharge or interfered with the employee's right to seek lawful employment or when the employer has breached an express or implied contract of employment.

12. A spouse can sue a third party for personal injury against the other spouse, as well as for alienation of affection and loss of consortium.

13. Malicious prosecution is the institution of criminal or civil proceedings without probable cause and with malice, that is, maliciously causing process to issue. Malicious abuse of process is the use of civil or criminal procedures for a purpose for which they were not designed, that is, improper use of process after it has issued.

14. The same elements of proof apply to trespass to real property as to personal property.

15. Four different circumstances that might constitute conversions are as follows:

(1) Acquisition of possession

(2) Unauthorized transfer of chattel

(3) Unreasonable withholding of chattel

(4) Damaging, altering, or misusing chattel

16. Jack's actions interfere with his neighbor's enjoyment of his or her property and constitute private nuisance.

17. Joe's act is a nuisance because it inflicts discomfort on his neighbors, unless Joe can prove that his music was not unreasonably loud.

Application Questions

1. A kidnapping usually would involve a threat of bodily harm, so assault is one tort the parents can allege. The kidnapper had to touch the child in some way to effectuate the kidnapping, so battery is another tort involved. The kidnapper also falsely imprisoned and unlawfully detained the child intentionally. Intentional infliction of emotional distress upon the parents (as well as the child) is another possible basis for suit. If the kidnapper entered the parents' property wrongfully, a trespass action might also be successful.

2. a. The surgeon has committed a battery upon the patient. This battery involved bodily contact without the patient's permission, and the patient's unconsciousness does not justify the lack of permission.

   b. Whether a tort has occurred depends on state law. A false imprisonment is the intentional and unlawful detention of one person by another. People detained for suspected shoplifting have sued successfully for false imprisonment, proving unreasonable detention. However, state statutes often permit detention for a reasonable time (usually an hour or less). Three hours may, in some jurisdictions, be considered an unreasonable time, resulting in the tort of false imprisonment.

   c. Sale of a stolen item, such as the car in this case, is conversion, the intentional and unlawful exercise of dominion or control over personal property to the detriment of the person entitled to control the property.

   d. The politician could sue for libel but might not be successful because the article saying the politician is suspected of bribery does not allege guilt of that crime and appears to assert only truth, and the politician is a public figure and therefore must prove the newspaper's malice to recover any damages—a difficult burden of proof.

   e. Jeff has committed malicious abuse of process, the use of legal procedures for a purpose for which they were not designed. Here Jeff is attempting to use coercion to acquire control over Scott's assets.

3. a. Jerry can sue the supervisor who has maligned him to others. The supervisor's assertions may be slander. The supervisor could use the defense that her assertions are true.

   b. Jerry can sue, but his suit might not be successful if the supervisor's assertions were true.

   c. Jerry can sue for the invasion of the right of privacy with regard to the allegation of alcohol abuse. His work performance, however, would not be a private matter. Therefore, if alcohol abuse affected his work performance and the supervisor can prove it, then Jerry's suit would fail.

4. Rob can sue the surgeon for invasion of privacy for public disclosure of private facts and unauthorized release of confidential information. Medical information also is subject to particularly strict rules of confidentiality.

5. Mikey's mother could sue for fraud because Jimmy's father did the following:
   - Deliberately concealed (falsely represented)
   - Material information
   - Knowingly,
   - With intent to influence or deceive,
   - Resulting in Mikey's and his parents' reasonable reliance
   - To their detriment.

   All elements of fraud exist here.

Direct Your Learning

Tort Law—Special Liability and Litigation Concepts

Educational Objectives

After learning the content of this assignment, you should be able to:

1. Describe the conditions for strict liability.

2. Given a products liability case, explain how liability is established for any of the following causes of action:

   a. Misrepresentation

   b. Breach of warranty

   c. Strict liability and negligence

3. Given a products liability case based on strict liability or negligence, explain what parties are potentially liable, what a defendant must prove to establish a defense, and what damages a plaintiff can recover.

4. Describe the legal bases for toxic tort and environmental damage claims and the coverage the CGL policy provides for such liability.

5. Given a tort case, describe the kinds of damages a court might award a plaintiff.

6. Given tort cases, explain whether any of the following concepts relating to litigation would apply:

   a. Joint tortfeasor's liability

   b. Expanded liability concepts

   c. Tortfeasor's capacity

   d. Vicarious liability

   e. Good Samaritan issues

   f. Class actions and mass tort litigation

   g. Statutes of limitations and statutes of repose

Study Materials

Required Reading:
▶ The Legal Environment of Insurance
  • Chapter 10

Study Aids:
▶ SMART Online Practice Exam
▶ SMART Study Aids
  • Review Notes and Flash Cards—Assignment 10

Outline

▶ **Strict Liability**

    A. Hazardous Activities

    B. Animals

▶ **Products Liability**

    A. Misrepresentation

    B. Breach of Warranty

    C. Strict Liability and Negligence

        1. Types of Product Defects

        2. Potentially Liable Parties

        3. Parties Protected

        4. Defenses

        5. Damages

▶ **Toxic Torts and Environmental Damage Claims**

    A. Statutes and Common Law

    B. Insurance Coverage

        1. Coverage Applications

        2. Policy Exclusions

▶ **Tort Litigation**

    A. Damages

        1. Types of Damages

    B. Liability Concepts

        1. Joint Tortfeasors

        2. Expanded Liability Concepts

        3. Tortfeasor's Capacity

        4. Vicarious Liability

        5. Good Samaritan Issues

        6. Class Actions and Mass Tort Litigation

    C. Statutes of Limitations and Repose

        1. Time Cause of Action Accrued

        2. Types of Suits

        3. Property Suits

        4. Infants and Incompetents

▶ **Summary**

Writing notes as you read your materials will help you remember key pieces of information.

Key Words and Phrases

Define or describe each of the words and phrases listed below.

Products liability (p. 10.3)

MacPherson doctrine (p. 10.4)

Strict liability, or absolute liability (p. 10.4)

Implied warranty of merchantability (p. 10.6)

State of the art (p. 10.12)

Scientific knowability (p. 10.12)

Passive negligence (p. 10.12)

Active negligence, or assumption of risk (p. 10.12)

Toxic tort (p. 10.14)

Environmental law (p. 10.14)

Superfund (p. 10.15)

Potentially responsible parties (PRPs) (p. 10.15)

Commercial general liability (CGL) policy (p. 10.16)

Occurrence-based policy (p. 10.16)

Nominal damages (p. 10.18)

Special damages (p. 10.19)

Loss of wages and earnings (p. 10.19)

General damages (p. 10.19)

Pain and suffering (p. 10.19)

Emotional distress (p. 10.19)

Bad-faith damages (p. 10.19)

Survival statute (p. 10.21)

Joint tortfeasors (p. 10.22)

Contribution (p. 10.23)

Enterprise liability, or industry-wide liability (p. 10.25)

Alternative liability (p. 10.25)

Market-share liability (p. 10.25)

Concert of action (p. 10.25)

Conspiracy (p. 10.26)

Family purpose doctrine (p. 10.27)

Mass tort litigation (p. 10.28)

Statute of limitations (p. 10.29)

Statute of repose (p. 10.29)

Review Questions

1. What were the common-law exceptions to the rule that a contractual relationship was necessary to sue for negligence relating to a product defect? (p. 10.3)

2. Explain the common-law liability of a person using or storing explosives. (pp. 10.4–10.5)

3. Distinguish between common-law liability for domestic animals and wild animals. (pp. 10.5–10.6)

4. Identify the five elements for a products liability lawsuit based on strict liability. (p. 10.7)

5. Describe the three major ways in which a product may be defective. (p. 10.8)

6. What parties in products liability cases can be strictly liable? (pp. 10.10–10.11)

7. Is the buyer the only party who can sue in strict liability? Explain. (p. 10.11)

8. Describe the defenses to a products liability claim. (pp. 10.12–10.13)

9. What is the primary purpose of CERCLA? (p. 10.15)

10. Identify the types of parties who might be liable under CERCLA. (p. 10.15)

11. What types of damages do compensatory damages include? (p. 10.19)

12. Describe the situations in which a plaintiff can recover punitive damages. (p. 10.20)

13. Contrast common law with UCAJTFA joint tortfeasor liability. (pp. 10.22–10.23)

▶▶

14. Identify three relationships that can be the basis of vicarious liability. (pp. 10.26–10.27)

15. What protection do Good Samaritan statutes provide? (p. 10.27)

16. When does a cause of action accrue for purposes of determining when a statute of limitations starts to run? (pp. 10.29–10.30)

17. When does a statute of limitations begin to run for an infant who is the victim of tort? (pp. 10.30–10.31)

Application Questions

1. Marla purchased a Weed Chopper, which is a powerful automatic weed cutter that was advertised as the "safest device on the market" for cutting weeds.

   a.   Whom does the law protect with regard to any safety problems with the Weed Chopper?

   b.   The Weed Chopper hits a rock and causes it to fly into the air, injuring Marla's neighbor's son, Denny. Can Denny sue the Weed Chopper manufacturer? Can he sue the store from which Marla bought the Weed Chopper?

   c.   For what might the Weed Chopper manufacturer be strictly liable, if anything?

2. Jack recently bought a gas station. He has discovered that the underground storage tank has been leaking gasoline into the ground for years.

   a.   Who must correct this situation?

b.   Can Jack sue anyone?

3. Sue has discovered a hazardous waste dumping site on her cattle ranch, which she purchased only six months ago. She has no idea who dumped the materials, which are medical wastes, on her land. However, the wastes appear to have been there for years. Her commercial general liability (CGL) policy has been in effect for only six months and is occurrence-based.

   a.   What are the legal issues Sue now faces, particularly with regard to her CGL policy?

   b.   Sue's guest, Ronny, believes he contracted a serious disease from accidental physical contact he had with the medical wastes dumped on Sue's ranch. What kinds of damages might he claim in a lawsuit? From whom?

4. A manufacturing plant discharges polluted water into a river. Pauline and Sarah each own land along the river. Pauline has a small factory that uses river water. The polluted water seriously damages Pauline's machinery. Sarah's property sustains only the damages that any abutting property would sustain. Pauline and Sarah each sue the manufacturer.

   a.   Does Pauline have a right of action? Explain.

b. Does Sarah have a right of action? Explain.

5. Jack, Carol, and Joe assault Tom in the dark without reason and seriously injure him. Tom's primary injury is a fractured skull caused by a single blow to the head. Tom did not know who of the three struck this blow. Tom's doctor and hospital bills amounted to $10,000 plus $25,000 for pain and suffering.

a. Can Tom sue Jack only? Explain.

b. Assuming that Tom can sue only Jack, can Jack involve Carol and Joe in the suit? Explain.

c. If Tom recovers the full $35,000 from Jack, what proportion of the judgment can Jack recover from Carol and Joe under common law? Under the Uniform Contribution Among Joint Tortfeasors Act (UCAJTFA)?

Answers to Assignment 10 Questions

NOTE: These answers are provided to give students a basic understanding of acceptable types of responses. They often are not the only valid answers and are not intended to provide an exhaustive response to the questions.

Review Questions

1. The common-law exceptions to the rule that a contractual relationship was necessary to sue were as follows:

    *   One who has marketed an inherently dangerous product that was also defective was liable to anyone injured because of the defect.

    *   A manufacturer who made, assembled, or sold a product not inherently dangerous, but that could be inherently dangerous if defective, was liable to any person injured while using the product in a reasonable manner.

    *   A manufacturer who was not only negligent in manufacturing a product, but who also knowingly concealed the defect, could be liable for both negligence and fraud.

2. At common law, a person using or storing explosives is strictly liable for all damages by the explosives.

3. At common law, owners of domestic animals are strictly liable for damages caused by the trespass of the animals but are strictly liable for injuries caused by the animal only if they knew of its dangerous propensity. Owners of wild animals are strictly liable for all acts and all damage caused by the animals.

4. The five elements required for a products liability lawsuit based on strict liability are as follows:

    (1) The seller was in the business of selling products.

    (2) The product had a defect that made it unreasonably dangerous.

    (3) The product was dangerously defective when it left the manufacturer's or seller's custody or control.

    (4) The defect was the proximate cause of the plaintiff's injury.

    (5) The product was expected to and did reach the consumer without substantial change in condition.

5. The three major ways in which a product might be defective are as follows:

    (1) Defect in manufacture or assembly—the product does not correspond to the original design.

    (2) Defect in design—the product corresponds to the design, and the manufacturer built the product exactly as intended, but the design itself is faulty.

    (3) Failure to warn—the product is defective in neither design nor manufacture, but it has some inherent danger about which the manufacturer has failed to give proper warning.

6. Parties that can be strictly liable are entities that engage in the business of selling products, distributors, wholesalers, retailers, bailors, lessors, builders, and contractors.

7. Protection can extend to the ultimate user or consumer, who might be different from the ultimate buyer, so the buyer is not the only party who can sue in strict liability.

8. The defenses to a products liability claim are as follows:
   - State-of-the-art defense, that the product was safe according to the state of the art at the time the product was made.
   - Compliance with statutes and regulations defense, that the product was up to standards based on statutes and regulations when the product was made. This is not a complete defense.
   - Compliance with product specifications defense, in which a manufacturer is generally not liable for products built to someone else's specifications unless the defect is sufficiently obvious to alert the manufacturer to the potential for harm.
   - Open and obvious danger defense, that the manufacturer has no duty to warn of obvious dangers.
   - Plaintiff's knowledge defense, that the product user had knowledge of the product that is equal to the manufacturer's knowledge.
   - Assumption of risk defense, that the person using the product had taken on the risk of loss, injury, or damage.
   - Misuse of product defense, that the plaintiff has not proved that the product was used in an appropriate and foreseeable manner.
   - Alteration of product defense, that the product was modified after it was sold.
   - Post-accident remedial measures defense, which prohibits a plaintiff's attempt to prove negligence by introducing evidence that the defendant took measures after an event that, if taken before the event, would have made it less likely to happen.
   - Written disclaimers, which manufacturers use to disclaim strict liability in some UCC breach of warranty situations. Most courts have rejected the validity of such disclaimers.

9. The primary purpose of CERCLA is to require the cleanup of hazardous waste disposal sites.

10. The types of parties who can be liable under CERCLA are as follows:
    - Current owners and operators of hazardous waste facilities
    - Past owners or operators of hazardous waste facilities
    - Generators of hazardous waste
    - Transporters of hazardous waste

11. Compensatory damages include both special and general damages.

12. A court may award punitive damages when the defendant intended to cause harm or when the defendant acted oppressively, maliciously, or fraudulently.

13. At common law, a release of one joint tortfeasor released all joint tortfeasors, even if the release specifically prohibited release of the other tortfeasors. Under the UCAJTFA, a plaintiff can release one or more defendants without releasing the others.

14. Three relationships that can be the basis of vicarious liability are as follows:
    (1) Principal and agent
    (2) Employer and employee
    (3) Parent and child

15. In most states, Good Samaritan statutes protect from liability any person who gives emergency assistance. Some states' Good Samaritan laws protect only medical personnel.

16. A cause of action accrues when all the elements of a basis for a right to sue occur.

17. A statute of limitations begins to run for an infant from the date the infant comes of age.

Application Questions

1. a. The law protects the buyer of a defective product, as well as the ultimate user and anyone else injured because of the use of the product. Most courts allow suits by nonusers, such as bystanders, or other strangers.

   b. In most states, Denny, a bystander, would be protected by law. Denny can sue both the store and the manufacturer, and a court would determine the relative liability (if any) of each.

   c. The Weed Chopper manufacturer can be strictly liable for product defects (faulty manufacture, assembly, or design) or for failure to warn of possible danger.

2. a. Jack must correct this situation because he faces potential liability even though he did not know about the underground tank when he purchased the gas station.

   b. Jack can sue the people from whom he bought the station and/or any previous owners who might be responsible for the leaking tank.

3. a. Sue's occurrence-based CGL policy would cover occurrences that have happened during the six months she has had the policy but would not cover wastes dumped there years ago. Even if the dumping had occurred within the policy period, an issue might arise as to whether the wastes were sudden and accidental discharges, the only covered pollutants under many CGL policies.

   b. Ronny might claim compensatory and special damages, loss of wages and earnings, intangible damages such as for pain and suffering and permanent injuries, damages for emotional distress, and punitive damages. Because this case involves hazardous waste dumping, CERCLA imposes liability potentially on Sue as the owner of the dump site, on past owners of the site, and on the generators and transporters of the polluting substances (if anyone can determine who they are).

4. a. Pauline can sue for nuisance on the ground that the pollution precludes her enjoyment of her property; for trespass on the ground that the pollutants constitute an unlawful entry onto her property; for negligence on the ground of negligent discharge of the pollutants causing damage to her machinery and business; and for strict liability if she claims the pollutants are hazardous substances.

   b. Sarah can sue for nuisance on the ground that the pollution precludes her enjoyment of her property; for trespass on the ground that the pollutants constitute an unlawful entry to her property by the defendant; for negligence on the ground of negligent discharge of the pollutants, damaging her property; and for strict liability if she claims the pollutants are hazardous substances.

5. a. Tom can sue only Jack if he wishes. He can choose to sue all the tortfeasors or any one of them. (Plaintiffs often have good reasons for choosing defendants. For example, a defendant might have moved to another state or might otherwise be missing.)

   b. Jack can bring Carol and Joe into the suit, or he can sue them on his own to obtain their proportionate shares of the damages. In summary, Jack does not have to pay the entire judgment against him (unless he was totally at fault).

c. At common law, Jack could be totally responsible for the damages if he is the only one Tom sues. Common law held that each tortfeasor was jointly and severally liable for the full amount of the damages. Under the UCAJTFA Jack would have a right of contribution from Carol and Joe. If Jack pays more than his pro rata share of the common liability, he can collect the excess over his fair share equally from Carol and Joe (not to be prorated between them). If, for example, Jack is liable for $10,000 of the $35,000, the remaining $25,000 would be split between Carol and Joe equally as their liabilities.

Direct Your Learning

Agency Law

Educational Objectives

After learning the content of this assignment, you should be able to:

1. Given a case, explain whether appointment, estoppel, or ratification created an agency.

2. Given a case, explain whether an agent has actual or apparent authority to act on a principal's behalf and how the principal can create agency relationships by actual or apparent authority.

3. Describe the following:

   a. Duties an agent owes to the principal

   b. Remedies a principal has for an agent's default or wrongdoing

   c. Duties a principal owes to the agent

   d. Remedies an agent has for a principal's default or wrongdoing

4. Describe the various means by which parties can terminate agency relationships.

5. Explain the following:

   a. Third-party rights and liabilities toward principals and agents

   b. A principal's rights against third parties

   c. An agent's rights against third parties

6. Describe the factors required for *respondeat superior* to apply and the torts that might make an employer liable for an employee's torts.

7. Given a case, explain whether workers are employees or independent contractors.

8. Given a case, explain whether an employer is liable for an employee's torts and what liability an employer may have for an employee's torts.

Study Materials

Required Reading:
▶ The Legal Environment of Insurance
   • Chapter 11

Study Aids:
▶ SMART Online Practice Exams
▶ SMART Study Aids
   • Review Notes and Flash Cards— Assignment 11

Outline

▶ **Agency Creation**

  A. Agency by Appointment

  B. Agency by Estoppel

  C. Agency by Ratification

▶ **Agent's Authority**

  A. Scope of Authority

    1. Actual Authority

    2. Apparent Authority

  B. Duty to Ascertain Scope of Authority

  C. Delegation of Authority

▶ **Duties and Remedies**

  A. Agent's Duties to Principal

    1. Loyalty

    2. Obedience

    3. Reasonable Care

    4. Accounting

    5. Information

  B. Principal's Remedies

  C. Principal's Duties to Agent

    1. Agreed-on Period of Employment

    2. Compensation

    3. Reimbursement for Expenses

    4. Indemnity for Losses

  D. Agent's Remedies

▶ **Agency Termination**

  A. Just Cause

  B. Lapse of Time

  C. Accomplishment of Purpose

  D. Revocation

  E. Renunciation

  F. Death or Incapacity

  G. Changed Circumstances

▶ **Third-Party Liabilities and Rights**

  A. Agency Contract Liability

    1. Third Party's Rights Against a Principal

    2. Principal's Rights Against a Third Party

    3. Agent's Liability to a Third Party

    4. Agent's Rights Against a Third Party

  B. Tort Liability—Employment

    1. Respondeat Superior

    2. Employees and Independent Contractors

    3. Scope of Employment

▶ **Summary**

Before starting a new assignment, briefly review the Educational Objectives of those preceding it.

Key Words and Phrases

Define or describe each of the words and phrases listed below.

Agency (p. 11.3)

Principal (p. 11.3)

Agent (p. 11.3)

Power of attorney (p. 11.4)

Agency by estoppel (p. 11.4)

Ratification (p. 11.5)

Actual authority (p. 11.6)

Express authority (p. 11.6)

Implied authority (p. 11.6)

Apparent authority (p. 11.7)

Ministerial duties (p. 11.8)

General lien (p. 11.13)

Special lien (p. 11.13)

Disclosed principal (p. 11.16)

Partially disclosed principal (p. 11.16)

Undisclosed principal (p. 11.17)

Master-servant relationship (p. 11.21)

Respondeat superior (p. 11.21)

Employee (p. 11.21)

Independent contractor (p. 11.23)

Review Questions

1. When must an agency contract be in writing to be enforceable?
   (p. 11.3)

2. What is the usual method for creating an agency relationship?
   (p. 11.3)

3. Explain how an agency by estoppel can be created even though
   the principal has done nothing to create an agency? (p. 11.4)

4. State the four conditions for ratification of an unauthorized
   contract. (p. 11.5)

5. How may business custom relate to an agent's scope of authority?
   Give an example. (pp. 11.6–11.7)

6. How does an agent's apparent authority arise? (p. 11.6)

7. Under what circumstances, if any, must a third party communicate directly with a principal to confirm an agent's authority? (pp. 11.7–11.8)

8. What are the three qualifications to the rule that an agent cannot delegate duties to others? (p. 11.8)

9. Discuss whether an agent can go into the same business as the principal. (p. 11.9)

10. Do unpaid agents owe a lesser standard of care to their principals than paid agents do? (p. 11.10)

11. Describe the following duties of an agent: accounting and information. (pp. 11.10–11.11)

12. Identify the remedies a principal has against an agent. (p. 11.11)

13. Distinguish between the principal's duty to reimburse and the duty to indemnify. (pp. 11.12–11.13)

14. How can an agency relationship terminate without either principal or agent acting to bring about the termination? (p. 11.14)

15. Name one exception to the general rule that notice of a principal's death is not necessary for third parties. (p. 11.15)

16. Does an agent's bankruptcy necessarily terminate the agency relationship? (p. 11.16)

17. Why is it not possible for the agent of an undisclosed principal to have apparent authority? (p. 11.17)

18. Describe the actions by a third party that would eliminate the third party's rights against a principal. (pp. 11.17–11.18)

19. Under what circumstances, if any, does an agent's failure to disclose the principal's identity to a third party constitute fraud? (p. 11.18)

20. Describe the bases for holding an agent liable to a third party. (pp. 11.18–11.19)

21. What three circumstances must be present for the application of the doctrine of *respondeat superior?* (p. 11.21)

22. Identify the seven tests generally used to determine whether an employment relationship exists. (p. 11.22)

23. List three exceptions to the rule that one who engages an independent contractor is not vicariously liable for the latter's torts. (p. 11.24)

24. What factors are important to determining whether a tort has occurred within the scope of employment? (p. 11.24)

25. Describe an employer's liability for an employee's negligent and intentional torts. (p. 11.26)

Application Questions

1. April has a power of attorney authorizing her to sell and convey Paul's building for $100,000. April enters into a contract with June, the buyer. The contract provides that the price is $100,000 and that Paul will take back a $60,000 mortgage. Is the contract binding on the principal? Explain.

2. Ed is the owner of a men's clothing store. Al is Ed's agent in charge of purchasing merchandise for sale. Ed has certain personal ideas about the merchandise to be carried. In addition to regular items usually stocked in such stores, Ed has included a line of perfumes, believing that his customers might like to pick up such a gift for their wives or friends. Ed, however, abhors denim in any shape or form and has instructed Al not to buy denim clothing.

   a.   What type of authority, if any, does Al have to purchase perfumes, regular men's clothing, or denim clothing?

   b.   Assume that Al purchases denim clothing from Ethel, who does not know about Ed's distaste for denim. Is Ed liable to Ethel for the purchase price?

3. Annie, the agent, and Pat, the principal, enter into a written agreement for the purchase of goods from Tom by Pat, payment due within thirty days. Annie did not disclose to Tom either the existence or identity of the principal, and she signed the contract as an individual. The contract was within Annie's actual authority. The goods were stolen from Annie, and Pat never received them. When Tom demanded payment from Annie, Tom learned of the principal's identity and that the goods had been stolen.

   a. If Tom decides to sue Annie for the agreed price of the goods, will Tom recover?

   b. If Annie told Tom, before entering the written contract, that she was an agent for Pat, will Tom recover?

4. Smith entered into a distribution agreement with XYZ Baking Company. The agreement provided that Smith would own and maintain a truck with the name, "XYZ Company," painted on it, followed by the words, "Owned and Operated by Smith." Smith was to sell only XYZ Baking Company's products by establishing a customer base, and he was to sell the goods at prices set by the company. Smith made a $500 security deposit with the company for "faithful performance of the agreement" and wore a baking company uniform. Smith was to receive commissions for his work. The agreement could not be transferred to another person without the baking company's consent. While driving the truck in the assigned territory during a usual work day, Smith negligently struck and injured a pedestrian.

   a. What are the pedestrian's rights, if any, against Smith?

b. What are the pedestrian's rights, if any, against the XYZ Baking Company?

5. Burt owned a bar. He hired Phyllis as a bartender and instructed her not to serve alcoholic beverages to intoxicated persons because such service was a criminal offense under state statute. While Burt was absent, Phyllis disregarded instructions and served an obviously intoxicated person, who later was involved in an automobile accident. On investigation, the police learned that the driver had consumed alcoholic beverages at Burt's bar. What, if any, is the criminal responsibility of Burt for the crime committed by Phyllis?

Answers to Assignment 11 Questions

NOTE: These answers are provided to give students a basic understanding of acceptable types of responses. They often are not the only valid answers and are not intended to provide an exhaustive response to the questions.

Review Questions

1. Agency contracts must be in writing if they are to last beyond a year.

2. The usual method for creating an agency relationship is by express appointment.

3. An agency by estoppel can be created if the principal's words or conduct cause a third person to reasonably believe that an agency exists.

4. The four requirements for ratification of an unauthorized contract are as follows:

    (1) The agent must have purported to act for the principal.

    (2) The principal must ratify the entire transaction.

    (3) The principal must ratify the agreement before the third party elects to withdraw from the agreement.

    (4) The principal must have all material facts available before the ratification is binding.

5. An agent may have implied authority based on business custom. For example, even though an agent may not have express authority to sell specific goods for a specific price, if the agent has customarily sold the same kind of goods for the same price, then the agent has implied authority to sell the most recently delivered goods for that price.

6. A principal does not grant apparent authority. Apparent authority arises because of a third party's reasonable belief that the agent has authority.

7. A third party must communicate directly with the principal to confirm the agent's authority if the agent acts in a way adverse to the principal's best interests.

8. The three qualifications to the rule that an agent cannot delegate duties to others are the following:

    (1) Ministerial duties

    (2) Customary appointments

    (3) Emergency appointments

9. The agent must not undertake any business venture that competes with or interferes with the principal's business because loyalty is one of the agent's implied fiduciary duties to the principal.

10. Unpaid agents do not owe a lesser standard of care to their principals than paid agents do, although they cannot be compelled to perform duties.

11. An agent must account to the principal for all the principal's property and money that come into the agent's possession. Additionally, an agent owes a duty to keep the principal informed of all facts relating to the agency.

12. Remedies a principal has against an agent are the following:

    *   In a suit for breach of an agency contract, or in tort for harm done, remedies may be transfer of improperly held property, or damages.

- If the agent is insolvent, the remedy may be transfer of the property or value of any benefit the agent received.

- An injunction prohibiting the agent from revealing trade secrets obtained during the course of employment or from competing with the principal after termination of employment in violation of an agreement not to compete.

13. Duty of reimbursement means a principal must reimburse an agent for any expenses necessarily incurred for the discharge of agency duties. Duty of indemnity means a principal must reimburse an agent for any losses or damages the agent has suffered arising because of the agency and incurred through no fault of the agent.

14. An agency relationship terminates without either principal or agent acting to bring about the termination when the specified time for which authority is granted lapses or when the purpose of the agency has been accomplished.

15. One exception to the general rule that no notice of the principal's death need be given to third parties is in the case of banking rules, under which a bank has authority to pay checks drawn on a depositor's account until it receives actual notice of death.

16. An agent's bankruptcy usually terminates the agency relationship.

17. By definition, an undisclosed agent is unknown to the third party, who therefore does not know the agent is acting as an agent. Because apparent authority is based on the third party's belief that an agent has the authority, it cannot arise if the third party is not aware of the agency.

18. When the third party learns of the principal's existence and identity and elects to hold the agent liable for the contract, the third party's rights against the principal are discharged.

19. An agent's failure to disclose the principal's identity to a third party constitutes fraud when the agent has represented to the third party that the contract is on the agent's behalf alone or that the agent represents someone other than the real principal.

20. The bases for holding an agent liable to a third party are as follows:
- Breach of warranty of authority—an agent acts for a principal even with no actual authority to do so. (If the principal ratifies the contract, the agent's liability for breach of warranty terminates.)
- Incompetent principal—the agent is personally liable for breach of warranty of authority when acting on behalf of a minor or a mentally incompetent person, if the third party was not aware of the principal's incapacity.
- Undisclosed and partially disclosed principals—if a third party has intended to contract with the agent and the agent purported to act personally and not for a principal, the agent must disclose both the existence and the identity of the principal.
- Agent's personal liability—an agent who voluntarily assumes responsibility for performing the agreement is liable for the principal's nonperformance.
- Agent's liability to account—if an agent can receive money from a third party and does not provide it to the principal, the principal can recover it in a suit against the agent.
- Agent's liability for torts and crimes—an agent is liable for fraudulent or malicious acts that harm a third party.

21. The three circumstances that must be present for the application of the doctrine of *respondeat superior* are as follows:

    (1) The employee has committed a wrong for which he or she can be liable.

    (2) The employer has retained the right to control the employee's physical conduct.

    (3) The employee has committed the wrong within the scope of the employment.

22. The seven tests generally used to determine whether an employment relationship exists are as follows:

    (1) What extent of control the parties' agreement specifies

    (2) Whether the worker is engaged in a distinct occupation

    (3) What skill the occupation requires

    (4) Who supplies the instrumentalities, tools, and place of work for the worker

    (5) What length of time the worker is employed

    (6) What method of payment applies

    (7) Whether the work is part of the employer's regular business

23. Three exceptions to the rule that one who engages an independent contractor is not vicariously liable for the latter's torts are as follows:

    (1) Employer's negligence

    (2) Nondelegable duty

    (3) Inherently dangerous activities

24. Factors that are important to determining whether a tort occurred within the scope of employment are as follows:

    - Did the employer authorize the act, or was the act incidental to an act the employer did authorize?
    - Was the act one that such employees usually perform?
    - When and where did the act occur, and what was its purpose?
    - To what extent did the parties intend to advance the employer's interests by performing the act?
    - Did the employer furnish the instrumentality by which the employee committed the tort?
    - Did the employer authorize the extent of departure from the usual method of accomplishing the act?
    - Did the act involve the commission of a serious crime?

25. For both intentional torts and negligence, the employer is responsible if the act was within the scope of employment. If the employee's tort is intentional, the employer is liable whether or not the employee intended to benefit the employer by the act.

Application Questions

1. April has a binding power of attorney, which gives her the power to sell and convey Paul's building. Whether she can require Paul to take back a $60,000 mortgage might depend on custom and usage involved in such real property sales. If she had implied authority to agree to such a mortgage, then the contract is binding on Paul.

2. a.   Al may have express authority to purchase perfumes and regular men's clothing if Ed has specifically instructed him as to those items. If he has not issued specific instructions, Al at least has implied authority to purchase these items because they are regularly stocked in the store. He has no authority to purchase denim clothing.

    b.   Ethel had no reason to believe that Al was doing anything out of the ordinary because denim clothing would appear appropriate to Ed's business. Ethel would be reasonable, therefore, in assuming that Al had authority to buy the denim, so Al's authority is apparent authority. Ethel could hold Ed liable for the purchase. (Ed's recourse is to fire Al and possibly to sue him for the cost of the denim purchased.)

3. a.   Pat was an undisclosed principal to Tom. Tom can sue Annie. If Tom wins the lawsuit, Annie can attempt to collect from Pat the amount of damages she was required to pay to Tom.

    b.   Tom can recover from Pat because Pat is, in this scenario, a disclosed principal.

4. a.   Smith was negligent in injuring the pedestrian, and the pedestrian can sue Smith individually, regardless of Smith's relationship to XYZ.

    b.   The pedestrian is more likely to be successful in a suit against Smith because XYZ has little physical control over Smith. Using the tests in the text, one could argue either way in this case. Whether XYZ had sufficient control over Smith to establish an employer-employee relationship is difficult to determine. If such a relationship exists, XYZ may be vicariously liable for Smith's negligence. However, it is more likely that Smith would be considered an independent contractor. Smith owned and operated his own truck even though XYZ's name was on it. Even though XYZ gave him a territory and prices, he controlled his own comings and goings and had responsibility for establishing his own customer base.

5. Generally, no one is responsible for another's criminal act. Burt had instructed Phyllis not to serve intoxicated persons, and (aside from statutory responsibility below) would not, under common law, be liable for Phyllis's criminal act. However, the statute casts a new light on the situation. The facts given here do not indicate the specific provisions of the statute in question, but generally a statute providing a criminal penalty imposes criminal liability upon the employer for the employee's illegally serving the alcoholic beverage. Thus, Burt probably would be liable under the statute.

Direct Your Learning

Agency Law: Insurance Applications

Educational Objectives

After learning the content of this assignment, you should be able to:

1. Describe the duties of the following:

   a. Producer

   b. Agent (general, special, or soliciting)

   c. Broker

2. Explain how to create producers' authority.

3. Describe the extent of producers' authority.

4. Explain how producers' authority can be terminated.

5. Describe producers' duties and liabilities to insurance customers, third parties, and insurers, as well as their claim settlement authority.

6. Describe errors and omissions coverage and an insurer's liability for a producer's acts and omissions.

7. Given a case, explain how to create a claim representative's authority, and justify your answer.

8. Describe claim representatives' duties to insurance customers, third parties, and insurers.

Study Materials

Required Reading:
▶ The Legal Environment of Insurance
  • Chapter 12

Study Aids:
▶ SMART Online Practice Exams
▶ SMART Study Aids
  • Review Notes and Flash Cards—Assignment 12

Outline

▶ **Insurance Producer Classifications**

A. Agents

B. Brokers

C. Producers' Authority

    1. Actual Authority

    2. Apparent Authority

D. Extent of Producers' Authority

    1. Producers' Status

    2. Producers' Notice and Knowledge

    3. Producer's Authority to Bind Coverage

    4. Appointment of Subagents

E. Termination of Producer Authority

F. Producers' Duties and Liability

    1. Duties and Liability to Insurance Customers

    2. Defenses to Liability

    3. Duties to Third Parties

    4. Duties and Liability to Insurer

G. Errors and Omissions Coverage

H. Insurer's Liability for Producer's Acts and Omissions

▶ **Claim Representatives**

A. Classification of Claim Representatives

B. Claim Settlement Authority

    1. Actual Authority

    2. Apparent Authority

C. Claim Representatives' Duties and Liability

    1. Duties to Insurers

    2. Duties to Insureds and to Third-Party Claimants

D. Claim Representatives' Personal Liability

▶ **Summary**

Perform a final review before your exam, but don't cram. Give yourself between two and four hours to go over the course work.

Key Words and Phrases

Define or describe each of the words and phrases listed below.

Insurance producer (p. 12.3)

Insurance agent (p. 12.3)

General agent (p. 12.4)

Special agent (p. 12.4)

Soliciting agent (p. 12.4)

Broker (p. 12.4)

Errors and omissions (E&O) liability policy (p. 12.13)

Default judgment (p. 12.32)

Staff claim representative (p. 12.33)

Independent adjuster (p. 12.34)

Public adjuster (p. 12.34)

Unfair claim settlement practices act (p. 12.39)

First-party bad-faith lawsuit (p. 12.40)

Excess liability (p. 12.42)

Review Questions

1. Who has the broadest authority of all agents to enter into insurance contracts? (p. 12.4)

2. What type of agent is typical of most of today's insurance agents? (p. 12.4)

3. What specific actions by an insurer could bind the insurer to the unauthorized acts of an insurance agent? (p. 12.5)

4. Give an example of a broker acting as an insurer's agent. (p. 12.7)

5. If a producer knows an insurance applicant is a bad risk, does the insurer-principal also know this? (p. 12.10)

6. In what two situations is an insurer not bound by the producer's knowledge? (p. 12.10)

7. Explain why oral insurance contracts are valid. (p. 12.12)

8. Can an agent delegate any agency duties to another person? (p. 12.13)

9. How does an insurance agency relationship terminate? (pp. 12.14–12.15)

10. What standard of care and skill is required of insurance producers? (p. 12.16)

11. If an insurance agent promises a customer a policy that the insurer later denies, can the customer sue the agent? (p. 12.18)

12. Explain the extent of an agent's duty to determine an insurer's solvency. (pp. 12.20–12.21)

13. Under what circumstances does an agent have a duty to advise a client about the client's insurance needs? (pp. 12.21–12.22)

14. Explain why an insured's failure to read the policy is not always an adequate insurer defense against liability. (pp. 12.26–12.27)

15. What right of action, if any, does an injured motorist have against a negligent motorist's insurance producer for failure to acquire liability insurance for the motorist? (p. 12.27)

16. What is the extent of a producer's liability to an insurer for failure to comply with the insurer's instructions to cancel a policy? (p. 12.31)

17. Is an insurer ever liable for a producer's errors and omissions? Explain. (p. 12.32)

18. Would a self-insured company most likely work with a staff adjuster or an independent adjuster? (p. 12.34)

19. What types of authority does an adjuster have to settle a claim? (pp. 12.35–12.37)

20. A claim adjuster tells an insured motorist involved in an accident, "We'll handle your claim." Does this statement bind the insurer to pay the claim? (p. 12.37)

21. An insurer gives an adjuster a manual that sets appropriate procedures for claim management. To which adjuster's duty does such a manual relate? (p. 12.38)

22. Who typically has authority to enforce state unfair claim settlement practices acts? (p. 12.40)

23. What damages can be recovered in a first-party bad faith lawsuit?
    (p. 12.40)

24. Why do most jurisdictions not allow personal lawsuits against
    claim representatives for alleged unfair claim settlement practices
    unless their actions were willful, intentional, or reckless?
    (p. 12.44)

Application Questions

1. Angela is a soliciting agent in an insurance agency. One day her boss,
   Helen, the general agent, stepped out of the office for about an hour.
   Angela answered Helen's phone. A worried customer on the line said
   tearfully, "My husband just had a very bad auto accident. I'm afraid
   we sent our premium a few days late. Are we covered?" Angela, who
   had originally procured this customer, said reassuringly, "Oh, I'm sure
   it's OK. Helen isn't here, but I'm sure everything will be all right."
   The customer breathed a sigh of relief and said, "I'd better get to the
   hospital."

   a. Did Angela bind the insurer?

   b. What is Angela's liability, if any?

    c.   What is Helen's liability, if any?

2. Sally, a life insurance soliciting agent, is informed by Albert, a life insurance applicant of facts that would cause the insurer either to reject Albert or increase his premium rate. Sally tells Albert about the problem, and Sally and Albert agree not to inform the insurer of the prejudicial facts. Is the insurer on notice of those facts on the theory that an agent's knowledge is imputed to the principal?

3. An insurer directed its agent to notify the insured under a particular policy that the insurer was canceling the policy. The insurance agent instructed the agency secretary to notify the insured. However, an allegation arose later that this notice was not effective to cancel the policy because an insurer's agent had not given it. Was this correct?

4. Karl asked Fred, an insurance agent, to obtain specific liability coverage. Because of an error, the written policy did not contain certain requested coverages. Fred was unaware of the error and delivered the policy to Karl, giving full assurance that the policy was written as requested. Karl did not read the policy. A loss occurred that the insurer would not cover. What, if any, is the liability of Fred and Karl?

5. José is an independent adjuster who adjusts claims sent to him by several insurers. For what activities toward settling the following claims can José incur reasonable expenses that will probably get insurer approval?

   a.   An auto collision in which two people suffered serious injuries

   b.   Destruction of a dwelling by a fire

Answers to Assignment 12 Questions

NOTE: These answers are provided to give students a basic understanding of acceptable types of responses. They often are not the only valid answers and are not intended to provide an exhaustive response to the questions.

Review Questions

1. A general agent has the broadest authority of all agents to enter into insurance contracts.

2. A special agent is typical of most of today's insurance agents.

3. An insurer can ratify the acts of an insurance agent who lacks the authority to bind the insurer and thus be bound.

4. If an insurer sends a broker numerous blank copies of its automobile policies and receives from the broker numerous copies of policies the broker has issued, the broker would be the insurer's agent by estoppel.

5. If a producer knows an applicant for insurance is a bad risk, that knowledge is imputed to the insurer.

6. In the following two situations, an insurer is not bound by the producer's knowledge:

   (1) When no actual agency relationship exists between the producer and insurer

   (2) When the agent has supplied false information

7. Oral insurance contracts are valid because the need for immediate insurance coverage arises frequently, and the lengthy underwriting process needed for a written contract is not time-efficient.

8. The general rule is that an insurance agent cannot delegate duties to another when the duties involve the producer's individual care, skill, and judgment. Other duties can be delegated to subagents.

9. An insurance agency relationship usually terminates under circumstances specified in the contract. The relationship can also terminate by an act of one of the parties that the other party might reasonably construe to show the intent to terminate.

10. An insurance producer must adhere to a standard of reasonable care and skill in relation to customers, who have little or no knowledge of insurance matters.

11. To sue the agent, the customer must prove that the producer agreed or undertook to obtain insurance coverage. An agent who assumes the obligation to procure insurance could be liable for not doing so; although, an agent who promised a policy, contacted the insurer on the customer's behalf, and then advised the customer of the insurer's decision not to provide coverage would have no liability.

12. The producer should make reasonable attempts to inquire into prospective insurers' solvency and should disclose to the customer any information revealing a weak financial condition.

13. An agent has a duty to advise a client about the client's insurance needs when the client has either inadequate or no insurance coverage for an unanticipated event or for an event the insured incorrectly believed was covered.

14. Some state courts do not allow this defense, reasoning that the customer has the right to rely on the producer's expertise and that policy language is often difficult to understand.

15. No. A third party who intends to sue an insurance customer cannot sue a producer who wrongfully failed to assist the customer in obtaining insurance coverage for the event that is the subject of the suit.

16. A producer who fails to comply with specific directions is liable to the insurer for the full amount of the loss the insurer must cover.

17. Sometimes the insurer becomes liable for the producer's acts or omissions, such as when a customer includes the insurer in a lawsuit, alleging that the producer acted on the insurer's behalf and is, therefore, responsible for the producer's conduct.

18. A self-insured company most likely would work with an independent adjuster.

19. An adjuster can settle a claim under implied authority when the adjuster reasonably believes that the insurer-principal wants the adjuster to take a certain action despite the lack of specific instructions. An adjuster also can settle a claim by express authority when following instructions in an employment agreement, a company manual, an insurer's memorandum, or a supervisor's verbal instructions.

20. A claim adjuster's statement to an insured motorist involved in an accident, "We'll handle your claim," does not, in itself, bind the insurer to pay the claim.

21. An insurer's manual that sets appropriate procedures for claim management relates to the adjuster's duty to follow instructions.

22. Typically, the state department of insurance enforces a state's unfair claim settlement practices act.

23. Damages for emotional distress and for attorney's fees, as well as compensatory damages, can be recovered in a first-party bad faith lawsuit. Sometimes punitive damages are also imposed.

24. The unfair claim settlement practices acts regulate insurers' conduct, and redress should be against the insurers. Only the insurer and the insured have a relationship under the insurance policy that is the subject of the claim, and the claim representative is not a party to that agreement.

Application Questions

1. a. Angela, as a soliciting agent, did not have the power to do anything beyond soliciting applications for insurance, forwarding them to the insurer, and performing other related activities. However, in this situation, it may not matter because, as to the worried customer, Angela has apparent authority to affirm that coverage is in effect. Although the customer probably would not keep her husband out of the hospital if Angela had replied negatively about coverage, she has relied on Angela's apparent authority. This question would not arise unless the insurer denied the claim. No evidence has appeared that the insurer has given any required notice of policy cancellation, and the payment was only "a few days late."

    b. If there is a real problem with coverage in this case, and the insurer places liability on Helen, then she could sue Angela.

    c. Helen is liable for Angela's exercise of apparent authority.

2. Sally and Albert have conspired to misrepresent information to the insurer. In so doing, Sally has abandoned her role as an agent and has committed fraud against the insurer, in league with Albert and in violation of her duty of loyalty to the insurer. The information Sally and Albert withheld is not imputed to the insurer.

3. Absent any state law to the contrary, the secretary's notification should be valid. She became an "agent of the agent" and had full authority to carry out the task as assigned.

4. As a result of his own negligence, Fred is liable to Karl for any loss that the insurer refuses to cover. The insurer was not at fault.

5. (a) & (b) For each claim, José can incur reasonable expenses connected with investigation, offers of settlement, releases, subrogation money collection, disposal of salvage, and inspection and appraisal of property.

Direct Your Learning

Employment Law

Educational Objectives

After learning the content of this assignment, you should be able to:

1. Describe the employment-at-will doctrine and its exceptions.

2. Summarize the laws prohibiting discrimination on the basis of each of the following:

   a. Age

   b. Sex, race, color, religion, or national origin

   c. Disability

3. Describe the laws that protect people who have served in the military, or on juries, or who face garnishment of wages.

4. Summarize the laws governing labor-management relations, collective bargaining, and economic pressure used in the collective bargaining process.

5. Given a case, apply the laws that regulate employee safety and health, wages and hours worked, and employee benefits, and justify your answer.

6. Given a case, apply the laws that protect employee privacy, and justify your answer.

Study Materials

Required Reading:
▶ The Legal Environment of Insurance
  • Chapter 13

Study Aids:
▶ SMART Online Practice Exams
▶ SMART Study Aids
  • Review Notes and Flash Cards—Assignment 13

Outline

▶ **Employment-at-Will Doctrine**

  A. Contract Claims

  B. Tort Claims

▶ **Antidiscrimination Laws**

  A. Discrimination Based on Age

    1. Age Discrimination in Employment Act (ADEA)

    2. Older Workers Benefit Protection Act

  B. Discrimination Based on Sex, Race, Color, Religion, or National Origin

    1. Civil Rights Acts of 1866 and 1871

    2. Civil Rights Act of 1964 (Title VII)

    3. Civil Rights Act of 1991

    4. Executive Order 11246

    5. Equal Pay Act

    6. Immigration Reform and Control Act of 1986

  C. Discrimination Based on Disability

    1. Americans With Disabilities Act

    2. Rehabilitation Act of 1973

  D. Other Areas Affected by Antidiscrimination Laws

▶ **Labor-Management Relations**

  A. Collective-Bargaining Relationships

  B. Collective-Bargaining Process

  C. Economic Pressure

▶ **Regulation of Employee Safety and Health**

  A. Duties of Employers and Employees Under OSH Act

  B. Safety and Health Standards Under OSH Act

  C. Enforcement and Penalties

▶ **Regulation of Wages and Hours**

  A. Fair Labor Standards Act

    1. Minimum Wage, Overtime, and Hours of Work

    2. Posting and Recordkeeping Requirements and Enforcement

  B. Other Federal Minimum Wage Acts

  C. Family Medical Leave Act (FMLA)

▶ **Regulation of Employee Benefits**

  A. Employee Retirement Income Security Act (ERISA)

  B. Consolidated Omnibus Budget Reconciliation Act (COBRA)

▶ **Employee Privacy**

  A. Employer Privacy Statutes

    1. Drugs and Alcohol

    2. Polygraph Tests

    3. Searches, Surveillance, and Background Checks

  B. Common-Law Invasion of Privacy

  C. Health Insurance Portability and Accountability Act (HIPAA)

▶ **Summary**

 study tips When reviewing for your exam, remember to allot time for frequent breaks.

Key Words and Phrases

Define or describe each of the words and phrases listed below.

Employment at will (p. 13.4)

Wrongful discharge (p. 13.4)

Bona fide occupational qualification (BFOQ) (p. 13.6)

Disparate treatment theory (p. 13.10)

Disparate impact theory (p. 13.10)

Quid pro quo sexual harassment (p. 13.11)

Hostile environment sexual harassment (p. 13.11)

Constructive discharge (p. 13.11)

Affirmative action plan (p. 13.13)

Yellow dog contract (p. 13.17)

Collective bargaining (p. 13.17)

Sit-down strike (p. 13.19)

Sympathy strike (p. 13.19)

General duty clause (p. 13.22)

Nonexempt employee (p. 13.24)

Exempt employee (p. 13.24)

Qualified beneficiary (p. 13.28)

Qualifying event (p. 13.28)

Review Questions

1. What tort claims can a dismissed employee make? (p. 13.5)

2. Can a company legally set a mandatory retirement age? (p. 13.6)

3. Which civil rights acts prohibit discrimination based on sex? On race? (pp. 13.8–13.9)

4. Distinguish between the disparate treatment and disparate impact theories of employment discrimination. (p. 13.10)

5. Distinguish between the quid pro quo and hostile environment types of sexual harassment claims. (p. 13.11)

6. Are sex-based insurance rates legal? (p. 13.12)

7. What are the most important features of the Civil Rights Act of 1991? (p. 13.12)

8. What does Executive Order 11246 require? (p. 13.13)

9. What does the Immigration Reform and Control Act require that employers verify with respect to their employees? (p. 13.14)

10. What conditions, other than physical disabilities, does the Americans with Disabilities Act cover? (p. 13.14)

11. What law prohibits an employer from discharging an employee because of garnishment of wages for indebtedness? (pp. 13.16–13.17)

12. Outline the process for establishment of the collective-bargaining relationship. (pp. 13.18–13.19)

13. What are examples of nonmandatory subjects for collective bargaining? (p. 13.19)

14. How can a group of employees apply economic pressure on an employer to strengthen its position? (p. 13.19)

15. How can an employer apply economic pressure to employees? (p. 13.20)

16. How does the OSH Act relate to the workers' compensation system? (pp. 13.20–13.21)

17. What are employer and employee duties under the OSH Act? (p. 13.22)

18. How is the OSH Act enforced? (p. 13.23)

19. What are the basic requirements of the Fair Labor Standards Act? (pp. 13.23–13.24)

20. Identify the rights of an employee under the Family and Medical Leave Act of 1993. (p. 13.26)

21. Does ERISA require employers to provide benefits to employees? Explain. (p. 13.28)

22. What does COBRA enable qualified individuals to elect? (p. 13.28)

23. What aspects of employee privacy are addressed by federal law? (pp. 13.29–13.30)

Application Questions

1. Ed, a thirty-eight-year-old plumber, did not have a written employment contract with his employer, Plumbing Company. However, he had worked there for twenty years, since the company first started in business. When he first started working there, the owner told him, "If you're a good plumber, you can work for us as long as we're in business." A week ago Ed's boss told him, "I'm afraid we'll have to let you go, Ed. Our business has fallen off, and we can't afford you anymore." Ed learned later that Plumbing Company had replaced him with a thirty-year-old plumber. The state in which Plumbing Company is located adheres to the employment-at-will doctrine.

    a. Does Ed have a contract claim against Plumbing Company?

b.   Does Ed have any other common-law claims against Plumbing Company?

c.   Does Ed have grounds for a discrimination lawsuit?

d.   Will Ed lose group health insurance benefits that the company had been providing for him?

2. Theatrical Company is recruiting actors and actresses for a staged production of a trilogy for children, including "Goldilocks and the Three Bears," "Little Red Riding Hood," and "The Gingerbread Man." The production has parts for the following characters: the three bears and Goldilocks; Little Red Riding Hood, her grandmother, her mother, the Big Bad Wolf, and a woodcutter; the gingerbread man, the little old lady and the little old man; several animals and plants; and a chorus. What parts might (or might not) legally require males or females as BFOQs?

3. Mark works for Insurance Company and prescreens businesses applying for commercial liability insurance. He gathers information about prospective insureds' financial condition, safety and health condition, and general compliance with legal requirements. He is currently examining Research Company and discovers the following conditions. Which of these conditions should he report as possibly violative of federal or state law? Which laws, if any, may apply?

a. Research Company is planning a reduction in work force and plans first to lay off those employees who are closest to retirement.

b. The second group of employees Research Company plans to lay off are those with the least seniority, most of whom are female and/or minority group members.

c. Research Company's main office building has steps leading to each entrance. One two-story building has no elevator.

d. Research Company's owner requires that all employees work five days a week, but on varying schedules that span weekends. For example, one employee might be off Tuesday and Wednesday, another Friday and Saturday. This scheduling keeps the research going at all times.

4. Mary and Al work for Garment Company. They are dissatisfied with their wages, hours, and benefits. The company employs 300 other workers.

   a. What must Mary and Al do to establish a collective bargaining unit?

   b. What subjects must Garment Company discuss with Mary and Al if they negotiate a collective bargaining agreement?

   c. If Garment Company is resistant, what actions can the employees take to exert economic pressure to get what they want?

5. Mary and Al fail in their attempts to form a union at Manufacturing Company. However, they still wish to improve conditions here.

   a. Mary works as a seamstress, and Al works as a fabric-sorter. Mary is paid less than Al, even though her work is substantially equivalent in most ways to Al's. Does she have a legal right to challenge this practice? If so, under what laws?

b. Mary and Al both believe that conditions at the company are unsafe. The upper two floors have no fire exits, and they believe storage of certain materials poses a fire hazard. What legal actions, if any, can they take to correct the situation?

c. The employees at Garment Company receive $4.50 an hour after $0.75 in mandatory "fees" are deducted, including a fee for aprons and a fee to cover employer-provided group bus transportation to and from work. They also work ten to twelve hours a day with only a half-hour lunch break and two ten-minute breaks at other times. What, if anything, can they do to improve their work conditions and wages?

Answers to Assignment 13 Questions

NOTE: These answers are provided to give students a basic understanding of acceptable types of responses. They often are not the only valid answers and are not intended to provide an exhaustive response to the questions.

Review Questions

1. A dismissed employee can make tort claims based on the following four causes of action:
   (1) Wrongful discharge
   (2) Intentional infliction of emotional distress
   (3) Defamation
   (4) Invasion of privacy

2. No, the ADEA bans mandatory retirement at any age.

3. Title VII prohibits discrimination based on sex. Section 1981 and the Civil Rights Act of 1991 prohibits discrimination based on race.

4. Under the disparate treatment theory, the employee must establish that the employer intended to treat individuals differently solely because of their sex, race, color, religion, or national origin. Under the disparate impact theory, the employer's intent is not an issue; the employee must show that apparently neutral employment practices applied equally to all individuals excluded a disproportionate number of a protected class under Title VII.

5. Quid pro quo sexual harassment deals with situations in which the job or job advancement is conditioned on submission to sexual advances. Hostile environment sexual harassment occurs when a person is exposed to abusive conduct or an otherwise hostile situation in the work area because of refusal to submit to sexual advances.

6. Sex-based insurance rates have been subject to legal challenge, but the law does not prohibit them.

7. The most important features of the Civil Rights Act of 1991 are as follows:
   - Amends Title VII and the ADA to allow plaintiffs to recover compensatory and punitive damages in discrimination suits
   - Broadens the scope of the Civil Rights Act of 1866 to apply to all aspects of the employment relationship
   - Changes the law regarding the burden of proof placed on each litigant in disparate-impact cases brought under Title VII or ADA
   - Makes jury trials available when plaintiffs seek compensatory or punitive damages under Title VII or ADA
   - Allows prevailing parties to recover expert witness fees

8. Executive Order 11246 requires government contracts to include specific nondiscrimination provisions.

9. The Immigration Reform and Control Act requires that employers verify the identities of their employees and their right to work.

10. Infectious diseases, mental illness, drug addiction, and alcoholism are disabilities within the ADA's terms.

11. The Consumer Credit Protection Act prohibits an employer from discharging an employee because of garnishment of wages for indebtedness.

12. To establish a collective-bargaining relationship, the representatives of both sides must meet at reasonable times and confer in good faith regarding employment conditions. If the subject matter is mandatory, refusal to bargain shows bad faith. Collective bargaining should result in a labor contract creating legally enforceable obligations between the parties.

13. Examples of nonmandatory subjects for collective bargaining are:
    * Right to subcontract work
    * Ballot clause requiring a secret ballot of all employees to consider the employer's last offer before calling a strike

14. Strikes, boycotts, and picketing are examples of how a group of employees can apply economic pressure on an employer to strengthen its position.

15. Employers can apply economic pressure to employees with replacement employees and lockouts.

16. The workers' compensation system provides an incentive for employers and insurers to engage in workplace safety activities. The OSH Act is a comprehensive law that provides for safety and health standards for the workplace and for employee protection, thereby reinforcing the system.

17. OSH Act requires employers to comply with safety and health standards promulgated under the act, maintain workplaces that are free from recognized hazards, and maintain records of employee injuries and illnesses. Employees under OSH Act are required to comply with occupational safety and health standards and all applicable OSH Act rules, regulations, and orders.

18. The OSH Act is enforced through workplace inspections and investigations by OSHA compliance officers.

19. The Fair Labor Standards Act establishes employment requirements relating to minimum wage, overtime compensation, child labor, and equal pay for men and women.

20. The rights of an employee under the Family and Medical Leave Act of 1993 involve wage compensation for absences resulting from birth, adoption, and care for an employee's own serious health condition or that of his or her spouse, child, or parent.

21. ERISA does not require employers to provide benefits to employees. An employer's obligations under ERISA arise only once the employer provides such a plan.

22. COBRA enables qualified individuals to elect continuation of group health insurance coverage for themselves and their dependents.

23. Federal law extends some protection to employees regarding drug, alcohol, and polygraph testing; searches and surveillance; and background checks.

Application Questions

1. a. Ed may have a contract claim despite the employment-at-will nature of the state law in his state. The owner's promise did not have to be in writing under the statute of frauds because it was possible that the contract could be performed within a year (the business could have ended within a year of the promise). However, even if Ed has a contract claim, his chances of success are questionable. Few courts would enforce an employment contract when business

necessity dictates cost-cutting. In employment-at-will states, it is difficult to enforce any kind of employment contract except one that is very clear-cut.

b. There is no evidence of any common-law claim Ed could make other than a contract claim unless Ed can prove the tort of intentional infliction of emotional distress. (No facts are provided that would support that tort.)

c. Ed is a male and has no cause of action for sex discrimination. He is thirty-eight and does not fall within the forty-years-of-age requirement for alleged age discrimination.

d. Under COBRA, Ed can remain on the group health policy for eighteen months after termination if he pays the premium. After that period, he would lose coverage. (COBRA applies only to a company having twenty or more employees working on 50 percent of an employer's working days during the preceding calendar year.)

2. None of these acting parts can legally require males or females as BFOQs. Actors of each gender can, with costumes and makeup, play each role.

3. a. The Age Discrimination in Employment Act (ADEA) and Older Workers Benefit Protection Act might apply to the older workers.

b. Title VII could be applicable in this situation as to alleged discrimination against women workers, and section 1981 could apply to racial discrimination of minorities.

c. The Americans with Disabilities Act (ADA) and Rehabilitation Act of 1973 would apply if the limited access situation causes problems for people with disabilities.

d. Title VII would apply to alleged discrimination based on religion.

4. a. Mary and Al must take the following steps:
- Pass out authorization cards to employees and request that they sign them.
- Ask the employer to bargain collectively. If the employer refuses recognition, the union can file an unfair labor practices charge.
- Alternatively, the union can file a representation petition with NLRB, and the NLRB will hold an election to certify the union.
- Mary and Al would also conduct a campaign to influence the workers.

b. Mary and Al must discuss the following subjects with the Garment Company:
- Wages, hours, and conditions of employment
- Merit wage increases
- Pensions
- Seniority rights
- Grievance procedures
- Management function clauses

c. The employees can exert economic pressure via strikes, boycotts, and picketing.

5. a. Mary can challenge the practice under the Equal Pay Act.

b. They can report the conditions to OSHA, requesting an inspection.

c. They can call the Department of Labor and report possible violations of the Fair Labor Standards Act (FLSA). The company is paying below minimum wage and might be violating the FLSA provisions regarding hours of work and breaks.

Direct Your Learning

Business Entities

Educational Objectives

After learning the content of this assignment, you should be able to:

1. Given a case, apply the legal characteristics of corporate structure.

   a. Explain how incorporation provides limited liability to corporate stockholders and what exceptions reduce that protection.

   b. Contrast the role of state and federal laws in regulating corporations.

   c. Explain how an organization's corporate powers are defined.

   d. Explain who in the corporate structure is responsible for liability for torts and crimes.

   e. Explain how corporations are formed and how corporate ownership is created.

   f. Describe the rights, powers, and duties of corporate stockholders, directors, officers, and employees.

   g. Describe the procedures by which corporate existence can terminate through merger, dissolution, and reorganization.

   h. Describe foreign corporations and their limitations.

2. Given a case, apply the legal characteristics of a partnership.

   a. Describe the forms of partnerships.

   b. Describe the authority and liability of individual partners to one another and to third parties for contracts, torts, and crimes committed by or on behalf of the partnership.

   c. Explain how a partnership can terminate.

3. Describe the purposes and functions of limited partnerships, limited liability partnerships, and limited liability companies.

4. Define the purposes and functions of unincorporated associations.

Outline

▶ **Corporations**

   A. Advantage of Incorporation

   B. Federal and State Laws and Regulations

   C. Corporate Powers

   D. Liability for Torts and Crimes

   E. Corporation Formation

      1. Promoters

      2. Incorporation

      3. Organizational Meeting

   F. Corporate Ownership

      1. Stated Capital

      2. Stock Rights, Warrants, Options, and Preemptive Rights

      3. Redemption or Purchase by the Corporation

      4. Stock Certificates

   G. Stockholders' Powers and Duties

      1. Right to Information

      2. Stockholders' Meetings

   H. Stockholders' Actions

   I. Board of Directors

      1. Number and Qualifications

      2. Meetings

      3. Committees

      4. Officers

   J. Duties of Directors and Officers

      1. Duties of Care and Loyalty

      2. Transactions With the Corporation

      3. Appropriation of a Corporate Business Opportunity

      4. Abuse of Minority Stockholders

      5. Liability and Indemnification

   K. Dividends

   L. Merger and Share Exchange

      1. Takeovers and Tender Offers

      2. Insurance Company Mergers

   M. Dissolution and Reorganization

   N. Foreign Corporations

      1. Licensing to Do Business

      2. Long-Arm Statutes

      3. Sarbanes-Oxley Act

▶ **Partnerships**

   A. Partnership Formation

      1. Joint Ventures

      2. Partnership by Estoppel

   B. Partnership Liability

      1. Tort Liability

      2. Criminal Liability

   C. Partners' Relationships to One Another

      1. Financial Relationship

      2. Fiduciary Relationship

      3. Partnership's Books and Property

      4. Assignment of Partner's Interest in Partnership

      5. Types of Decisions and Consent Required

   D. Relationship of Partners to Third Parties

      1. Apparent Authority (Estoppel) of Partners

      2. Acts Outside the Usual Scope of Business

      3. Ability to Convey Real Property

      4. Spouses' Rights in Real Property

   E. Dissolution, Winding Up, and Termination

      1. Rightful and Wrongful Dissolution

      2. Winding Up the Partnership Business

      3. Effect of Dissolution on Third Parties

   F. Limited Partnerships and Limited Liability Partnerships

   G. Limited Liability Companies

▶ **Unincorporated Associations**

   A. State Regulation of Associations

   B. Types of Associations

   C. Formation and Financing

      1. Articles of Association and Bylaws

      2. Rights of Members in Association Property

      3. Directors or Trustees

   D. Liability of Members to Third Parties

   E. Dissolution and Winding Up

▶ **Summary**

Key Words and Phrases

Define or describe each of the words and phrases listed below.

Corporation (p. 14.4)

Pierce the corporate veil (p. 14.4)

Publicly held corporation (p. 14.5)

Privately held corporation, or close corporation,
or closely held corporation (p. 14.5)

Foreign corporation (p. 14.6)

Alien corporation (p. 14.6)

Runaway corporation statute (p. 14.6)

Professional corporation (PC) (p. 14.7)

Corporate charter, or articles of incorporation (p. 14.7)

Ultra vires (p. 14.8)

Promoter (p. 14.9)

Incorporator (p. 14.10)

Certificate of incorporation (p. 14.10)

De jure (in law) corporation (p. 14.10)

De facto (in fact) corporation (p. 14.10)

Organizational meeting (p. 14.10)

Debt security, or bond (p. 14.11)

Equity security, or stock (p. 14.11)

Common stock (p. 14.11)

Preferred stock (p. 14.11)

Par value (p. 14.11)

Dissolution (p. 14.12)

Stated capital (p. 14.12)

Capital surplus (p. 14.12)

Stock right (p. 14.12)

Stock warrant (p. 14.12)

Stock option (p. 14.12)

Preemptive right (p. 14.12)

Redemption (p. 14.13)

Shareholder derivative suit (p. 14.14)

Proxy (p. 14.15)

Record date (p. 14.15)

Quorum (p. 14.15)

Cumulative voting (p. 14.16)

Voting trust (p. 14.16)

Direct action (p. 14.17)

Inside director (p. 14.18)

Outside director (p. 14.18)

Chief executive officer (CEO) (p. 14.19)

Chief operating officer (COO) (p. 14.20)

President (p. 14.20)

Vice president (p. 14.20)

Treasurer (p. 14.20)

Secretary (p. 14.20)

Interlocking directors (p. 14.21)

Insider information (p. 14.21)

Indemnification (p. 14.23)

Dividend (p. 14.24)

Property dividend (p. 14.24)

Stock dividend (p. 14.24)

Liquidating dividend (p. 14.24)

Capital gains (p. 14.24)

Treasury stock (p. 14.24)

Stock split (p. 14.25)

Corporate merger (p. 14.25)

Share exchange (p. 14.25)

Takeover (p. 14.26)

Tender offer (p. 14.26)

Insolvency (p. 14.27)

Long-arm statute (p. 14.28)

Service of process (p. 14.29)

Partnership (p. 14.29)

Joint venture (p. 14.30)

Common name statute (p. 14.31)

Limited partnership (p. 14.41)

Limited liability partnership (p. 14.41)

Unincorporated association (p. 14.42)

Review Questions

1. Identify and explain the exceptions to the limited liability of corporate stockholders. (pp. 14.4–14.5)

2. Identify what articles of incorporation typically contain. (p. 14.7)

3. How can a corporation's purpose be simply stated? (p. 14.7)

4. Is the officer of a corporation responsible for an employee's
   job-related criminal activity? Explain. (p. 14.9)

5. What duties, if any, does a promoter owe to the corporation
   the promoter is forming, to creditors of that corporation, and to
   fellow promoters? (p. 14.9)

6. Who, if anyone, can attack the validity of a *de facto* corporation?
   (p. 14.10)

7. Describe four typical bylaw provisions. (p. 14.11)

8. What preferences over common stocks do preferred stocks generally enjoy? (p. 14.11)

9. Describe stockholders' rights and powers. (p. 14.14)

10. Under what circumstances, if any, can stockholders be denied the right to inspect their corporation's books and records? (pp. 14.14–14.15)

11. What type of decisions made by a board of directors must stockholders approve? (p. 14.17)

12. In what ways are outside directors valuable? (p. 14.18)

13. What are corporate officers' functions? (p. 14.19)

14. Under what circumstances can a director contract with a corporation? (p. 14.21)

15. What are the penalties for insider trading? (p. 14.22)

16. What are the duties of directors and officers who manage an employee benefit plan under the Employment Retirement Income Security Act of 1974? (p. 14.23)

17. Why is distribution of assets not a dividend? (p. 14.24)

18. How do tender offers accomplish hostile takeovers? (p. 14.26)

19. Under what circumstances might an involuntary dissolution occur? (p. 14.27)

20. What is the purpose of long-arm statutes? (p. 14.28)

21. In what name or names can a partnership be sued? (p. 14.31)

22. Describe the financial and fiduciary relationships among partners. (pp. 14.32–14.33)

23. What is the managing partner's role? (p. 14.35)

24. Explain the extent of the power of a partner to convey real property to a third person under the UPA. (p. 14.37)

25. How are partnership assets distributed upon dissolution? (p. 14.39)

26. What is the purpose of a limited partnership? (p. 14.41)

27. Compare the limited liability company with (a) corporations and (b) partnerships. (p. 14.42)

28. List six types of unincorporated associations. (pp. 14.43–14.44)

Application Questions

1. Eric, an engineer, was introduced to Douglas, a director of APB Corporation. Douglas was very impressed by Eric and indicated that APB Corporation could use Eric's services. Douglas and Eric had a series of meetings, and Douglas finally made Eric a very attractive offer. Eric accepted and immediately resigned from his current position. When Eric reported to work at the APB Corporation, he was informed that the board of directors had voted not to approve Douglas's contract with Eric.

   a. What rights, if any, does Eric have against APB Corporation?

   b. To what extent, if any, would your answer to (a) change if Eric had made the contract with Paul, the president and chief executive officer of APB Corporation? Assume Paul had no express authority from the board to hire Eric.

2. Carol is president of X Corporation, a food business. The Food and Drug Administration inspected one of the corporation's warehouses and found evidence of rodent infestation. An order was issued to X Corporation to remedy the violation. Carol immediately instructed subordinates to carry out the order. Two months later, the FDA made another inspection, found that the violation still existed, and issued another order. Carol again instructed the subordinates to obey the order. After the third inspection, when the violation still existed, the FDA had a criminal action filed against the corporation and Carol. Is Carol, the corporation, or both criminally liable for the continued violation? Explain.

3. J.P. is the president and chief executive officer of a corporation. He owns 11 percent of the company stock. J.P. knows of a secret project that is close to success and will give the corporation a great advantage over its competitors. He is sure that the market price of its shares will rise significantly when the success of the project is announced. J.P. is thinking about borrowing on the security of his present holdings of that stock and buying 1,000 shares on the open market.

   a.   What legal issue(s) might arise if J.P. buys the shares?

   b.   Assume, for the purpose of this subpart, that J.P. bought the shares on January 15 and sold them at a profit on March 15 of the same year. Explain the consequences, if any, of J.P.'s action.

4. Ricardo and his three daughters formed a general partnership to manage certain real estate. Ricardo was the manager of the partnership and the only partner who took an active part in the conduct of the partnership business. He was taking $1,000 per month from the business as compensation for his management work. The three daughters sued for a partnership accounting, claiming that Ricardo was not entitled to such compensation for his services. Discuss the merits of the daughters' contention.

Answers to Assignment 14 Questions

NOTE: These answers are provided to give students a basic understanding of acceptable types of responses. They often are not the only valid answers and are not intended to provide an exhaustive response to the questions.

Review Questions

1. Several states hold stockholders liable for employees' wages and unemployment benefits earned, but unpaid, before a corporation's insolvency. Courts also make exceptions by holding stockholders liable for a corporation's wrongful acts, usually when a corporation forms for an illegal purpose. If stockholders ignore the corporation's separate identity, so will courts. Finally, inadequate capitalization can defeat a corporation's limited liability.

2. Articles of incorporation typically contain the following items:
    *   Corporate name
    *   Duration
    *   Purpose
    *   Number, classes, and par value of shares
    *   Provisions for the stockholders' right to purchase a proportionate share of a newly authorized stock issue
    *   Provisions restricting the transferability of shares
    *   Registered office and registered agent
    *   Number, names, and addresses of the initial board of directors
    *   Names and addresses of incorporators

3. Most states permit a corporate charter to describe its purpose as simply "for any lawful purpose."

4. Under statutes that impose criminal liability for unintentional acts, an officer can be criminally responsible for failure to ensure that subordinates comply with the statute.

5. Promoters have a fiduciary duty of the utmost good faith in dealing with one another and with the corporations they are organizing.

6. Only the state can legally challenge the existence of a *de facto* corporation.

7. Four typical bylaw provisions are as follows:
    (1) Stockholders' meetings—date, place, proxies, conduct of elections, order of business
    (2) Directors—term of office, compensation, meetings, loans, and authority to elect officers
    (3) Officers—names and functions, appointment, removal, authority to sign checks and enter contracts
    (4) Indemnification of directors, officers, and agents—provides for corporate reimbursement for individuals' liability

8. Preferred stock has priority over common stock, usually regarding dividends and capital distribution if the corporation ends its existence.

9. Stockholders have the power to elect board members, to remove them without cause in many states, and to approve changes in the articles of incorporation. They can make or amend bylaws and approve loans to the corporation's directors, officers, or agents. Stockholders can ratify board actions, and they can sue the directors for mismanagement. They have a right to their corporation's financial statements and the right to attend stockholders' meetings.

10. Stockholders can be denied the right to inspect their corporation's books and records if they hold less than a specified percentage of outstanding shares or have held stock for less than a specified period.

11. Amendments to the articles of incorporation, such as changes in the corporation's capital structure and form, require stockholder approval, as do decisions to merge, consolidate, or dissolve the corporation.

12. Outside directors can provide perspectives on the corporation's activities that those involved in day-to-day management might not have.

13. Corporate officers generally have one or both of the following functions:
    (1) Managing the corporation's internal affairs
    (2) Dealing with persons outside the corporation

14. A director can enter into a contract with a corporation if any of the following is true:
    - The material facts and relationship or interest were known or disclosed to the board, and the board approved it.
    - The material facts and relationship or interest were known or disclosed to the stockholders, and the stockholders consented.
    - The contract was fair to the corporation.

15. If officers or directors engage in insider trading, a court can award damages to the stockholder from whom the shares were purchased, the corporation can take the profit, or the U.S. Treasury can take three times the profit.

16. Directors and officers who manage an employee benefit plan under the Employment Retirement Income Security Act of 1974 have an obligation to act solely in the plan participants' interest, to exercise reasonable care and skill, to diversify investments unless it is clearly unreasonable to do so, and to act in accordance with the plan documents.

17. Distribution of assets is not a dividend because dividends come out of earnings, not assets.

18. In a tender offer, the acquiring corporation offers to purchase shares directly from the target company's stockholders.

19. State involuntary dissolutions occur in cases of gross abuse. Stockholders request involuntary dissolutions in the following circumstances:
    - The directors are deadlocked, the stockholders cannot break the deadlock, and irreparable injury to the corporation either has occurred or might occur.
    - The directors' and officers' acts are illegal, oppressive, or fraudulent.
    - The stockholders are deadlocked in voting power and have failed to elect directors for two successive meetings.
    - The corporate assets are being wasted or misapplied.

20. Long-arm statutes enable states' citizens to sue in their own state courts people or entities who are not physically present in the state but who have had minimum contacts there.

21. A partnership can be sued as a partnership in name or as the names of each partner individually.

22. The financial relationship among partners provides that each partner share equally in the enterprise's profits and in any surplus that remains on dissolution and after satisfaction of all liabilities. Every partner has a fiduciary relationship with the other partners and with the firm, requiring duties of mutual trust, loyalty, and good faith similar to those of an agent or trustee.

23. Managing partners are appointed to make all long-range policy decisions.

24. If the property is held under the partnership's name, any partner can transfer real property in the firm's name by signing a deed, and the partnership is bound unless the partner lacked actual authority to sell the property and the purchaser knew this fact.

25. If the partnership is solvent at the time of dissolution, the parties share in any surplus remaining after payment of debts and partners' equity. If it is insolvent, they share the losses.

26. A limited partnership is best suited to a temporary enterprise requiring a large amount of capital and having general partners who are good managers.

27. a. LLCs provide the limited liability of a corporation to all owners or members of the business.

    b. LLCs offer the tax advantages of a partnership.

28. The six types of unincorporated associations are:

    (1) Trade associations

    (2) Labor unions

    (3) Benevolent and fraternal associations

    (4) Religious organizations

    (5) Clubs

    (6) Condominium owners' associations

Application Questions

1. a. Eric can sue APB for breach of a contract. Eric relied on the contract to his detriment. The corporation might dispute the director's authority to hire and to contract with Eric, but Eric's recourse is against the corporation.

    b. Paul, as CEO, would have the authority to hire personnel and to represent APB in this process. He is an agent for the corporation and acted as such in hiring Eric. As CEO, Paul would not have needed express authority from the board to hire Eric. In either instance, (a) or (b), Eric's recourse is against the corporation.

2. Carol gave specific instructions to her subordinates, but they disobeyed her and the law. This form of violation may be strict liability, that is, lack of intent would be immaterial. Even though the subordinates acted independently, disobeying Carol as the company representative, the company is criminally liable. A corporation may be responsible for an employee's criminal activity if it could have uncovered the activity through reasonably diligent supervision, which is probably the case here. Officers and employees who commit crimes are personally responsible for those crimes. Carol, as well as the corporation, would be criminally liable because she failed to effect her subordinate's compliance.

3. a. J.P. might be in violation of his legal duties to the corporation. He cannot use material information obtained through his duties in deciding to buy or sell the corporation's stock. The shareholders can sue him for use of insider information.

    b. He is guilty of illegal use of insider information under the Insider Trading Sanctions Act of 1984 and faces three liabilities:

        (1) Damages to the stockholder/s from whom the share was purchased

        (2) Corporate seizure of his profits

        (3) Forfeiture of up to three times the profit to the U.S. Treasury

4. The daughters might prevail if they can prove that they did not authorize the father's compensation. No partner is entitled to remuneration for services unless the partners agree to it.

 If you find your attention drifting, take a short break to regain your focus.

Direct Your Learning

The International Legal Environment of Insurance

Educational Objectives

After learning the content of this assignment, you should be able to:

1. Summarize the history of international business and the growth of multinational companies.

2. Given a case, recommend a method for a company to enter the international business markets based on foreign trade, foreign contractual relationships, and/or foreign direct investments.

3. Describe the challenges and barriers facing international companies.

4. Compare the predominant legal systems: civil law (Roman/French, German, Scandinavian [Nordic]), common law, Far Eastern, Hindu Islamic, and socialist/communist.

5. Describe issues in public and private international law that affect international transactions.

6. Describe the insurers and brokers leading the international insurance markets.

7. Summarize the following financial considerations in international insurance:

    a. Currency and foreign exchange markets

    b. Expropriation

    c. Accounting issues

    d. Taxation issues (including the formation and benefits of tax havens)

8. Explain how significant areas of the U.S. Internal Revenue Code (IRC), the Foreign Corrupt Practices Act (FCPA), and the Patriot Act influence international business and foreign investment.

9. Summarize the roles and/or responsibilities of prominent multinational organizations and agreements in influencing the direction and development of world business.

Study Materials

Required Reading:
▶ The Legal Environment of Insurance
  • Chapter 15

Study Aids:
▶ SMART Online Practice Exams
▶ SMART Study Aids
  • Review Notes and Flash Cards—Assignment 15

Outline

▶ **International Business**

  A. Foreign Trade

    1. Absolute and Comparative Advantage

    2. U.S. Trade in the World Context

  B. Foreign Contractual Relationships

    1. Product Licensing

    2. Franchising

  C. Foreign Direct Investments

    1. Subsidiaries

    2. Joint Ventures

  D. Challenges and Barriers

    1. Language

    2. Culture

    3. Time

    4. Distance and Space

    5. Types of Governments

▶ **Legal Systems**

  A. Civil Law

    1. Roman-French Law

    2. German Law

    3. Scandinavian Law

  B. Common Law

  C. Far Eastern Law

  D. Hindu Law

  E. Islamic Law

  F. Socialist-Communist Law

▶ **International Law**

▶ **International Insurance Markets**

  A. The Players—Insurers

  B. The Players—Insurance Brokers

▶ **Financial Considerations in International Insurance**

  A. Currency and Foreign Exchange Markets

  B. Expropriation

  C. Accounting Issues

  D. Taxation Issues

▶ **U.S. Law**

  A. Tax Code

  B. Foreign Corrupt Practices Act

  C. The Patriot Act

▶ **Multinational Organizations and Agreements**

  A. United Nations (UN)

  B. World Trade Organization (WTO)

  C. North American Free Trade Agreement (NAFTA)

  D. European Union (EU)

  E. Association of Southeast Asian Nations (ASEAN) and ASEAN Free Trade Area (AFTA)

  F. Asia-Pacific Economic Cooperation (APEC)

▶ **Summary**

Studying before sleeping helps you retain material better than studying before undertaking other tasks.

Key Words and Phrases

Define or describe each of the words and phrases listed below.

Business risk (p. 15.5)

Absolute advantage (p. 15.5)

Comparative advantage (p. 15.5)

Product licensing (p. 15.7)

Franchising (p. 15.7)

Foreign direct investment (p. 15.8)

Foreign portfolio investment (p. 15.8)

Subsidiary (p. 15.8)

Resource seeker (p. 15.9)

Market seeker (p. 15.10)

Market follower (p. 15.10)

Democratic rule (p. 15.13)

Nonparty democracy (p. 15.13)

Parliamentary democracy (p. 15.13)

Presidential democracy (p. 15.13)

Multiparty democracy (p. 15.14)

Junta (p. 15.14)

Martial law (p. 15.14)

Monarchy (p. 15.14)

Absolute monarchy (p. 15.14)

Constitutional monarchy (p. 15.14)

Single-party government (p. 15.14)

Theocratic government (p. 15.14)

Transitional government (p. 15.14)

International law (p. 15.21)

Public international law (p. 15.21)

Private international law (p. 15.21)

Comity (p. 15.22)

Pegged currency (p. 15.27)

Expropriation (p. 15.28)

Territorial tax system (p. 15.29)

Worldwide tax system (p. 15.29)

Border tax adjustment (BTA) (p. 15.30)

Earnings stripping (p. 15.30)

Inversion, or expatriation, or reincorporation (p. 15.30)

Transfer price (p. 15.30)

Tax haven (p. 15.30)

Bearer share (p. 15.32)

Registered share (p. 15.32)

Repatriation of earnings (p. 15.33)

Foreign sales corporation (FSC) (p. 15.34)

Extraterritorial Income (ETI) (p. 15.34)

Dumping (p. 15.41)

Common Market (p. 15.44)

Euro (p. 15.44)

Review Questions

1. Compare the concepts of absolute and comparative advantage. (p. 15.5)

2. Identify the three reasons for the licensing of products between different countries. (p. 15.7)

3. When does franchising occur? (p. 15.7)

4. What kind of subsidiary provides a company with the highest level of control over operations? What is the disadvantage of this kind of subsidiary? (p. 15.8)

5. Distinguish resource seekers, market seekers, and market followers as the terms are used in the text. (pp. 15.9–15.10)

6. Identify the challenges facing companies engaging in international business. (pp. 15.11–15.15)

7. Identify the two major legal systems. (p. 15.15)

8. What are the three stages of a typical civil-law case? (p. 15.16)

9. Describe a common-law system. (p. 15.18)

10. Contrast public and private international law. (p. 15.21)

11. What is comity of nations? (p. 15.22)

12. Identify the two segments of the national insurance industry.
    (p. 15.23)

13. What are the financial considerations in the international insurance market? (p. 15.26)

14. Contrast expropriation and eminent domain. (p. 15.28)

15. Identify the different approaches to taxing a corporation's earnings in the context of international commerce. (p. 15.30)

16. What should a business consider when establishing a subsidiary in an offshore tax haven? (p. 15.31)

17. What is repatriation of earnings? (p. 15.33)

18. Identify five U.S. laws changed by the Patriot Act. (p. 15.36)

19. What are the United Nations' purposes? (p. 15.38)

20. Identify the three primary WTO agreements. (p. 15.41)

21. To what countries does NAFTA apply? (p. 15.42)

22. What effect does, or will, NAFTA have on tariffs? (p. 15.43)

23. What is the ASEAN? (pp. 15.44–15.45)

24. What is APEC? (p. 15.45)

Application Questions

Facts: Farm Insurance Company (FIC), with ninety years of experience specializing in farm-related insurance coverages in the midwestern United States, has decided that the time has come to export its farm insurance products abroad by becoming a global competitor in the farm insurance business. FIC's plan includes going into developing countries that currently do not have any similarly specialized insurers.

1. An international business consultant has advised FIC that its best choices for globalizing are (a) to own a subsidiary in each country or (b) to enter a joint venture in each country. Discuss the advantages and disadvantages of each option.

2. FIC is investigating doing business in Peru and Liberia. Identify the challenges FIC might face in each of these countries.

3. FIC has hired a consulting firm to explore taxation issues in various countries. What should the company research about these three countries—Peru, Liberia, and Uzbekistan—to determine if they might be tax havens?

Answers to Assignment 15 Questions

NOTE: These answers are provided to give students a basic understanding of acceptable types of responses. They often are not the only valid answers and are not intended to provide an exhaustive response to the questions.

Review Questions

1. A country has absolute advantage when it specializes in goods or services more efficiently and trades them for the goods and services it produces less efficiently. A comparative advantage occurs when trading partners gain from trading with each other even when they are themselves more efficient in production of the traded goods and services.

2. The licensing of products between different countries can occur for the following three reasons:

   (1) A company might decide that it is not economically viable to sell its product in the second country because of labor costs, transportation costs, or regulations.

   (2) A company might decide that it does not have the time or resources to produce the product in another country.

   (3) A company might lack sufficient knowledge about the country's legal, political, social, and business environments.

3. Franchising occurs when one company assigns to another the right to supply its products within a market.

4. A fully owned subsidiary provides a company with the highest level of control over operations. The disadvantage of this kind of subsidiary is that it presents the highest level of business risk, commitment of capital, and managerial control.

5. Resource seekers are companies that enter a foreign market seeking that country's resources. Market seekers are companies that seek new markets outside their own countries' boundaries. Market followers follow their customers into foreign countries.

6. The challenges facing companies engaging in international business include the language barrier, cultural differences, time differences between countries, physical distance and space between countries, and government structure.

7. The two major legal systems in the majority of countries are the civil-law system and the common-law system.

8. The three stages of a typical civil-law case are the following:

   (1) The preliminary stage

   (2) The evidence stage

   (3) The decision stage

9. In the common-law legal system, a judge interprets the facts of a case, examines precedents, and makes a decision based on the facts in the current case.

10. Public international law concerns the interrelation of nation states and is governed by treaties and other international agreements, while private international law is national law that involves disputes between individuals or corporations in different countries.

11. Comity of nations is the courtesy by which one country recognizes, within its own territory or in its courts, another country's institutions.

12. The two segments of the national insurance industry are life insurance and nonlife insurance.

13. Some financial considerations in the international insurance market are the following:
    - Currency and foreign exchange markets
    - Expropriation
    - Accounting issues
    - Taxation issues

14. Expropriation is a government's lawful acquisition of property without the owner's consent, and often without compensation. The government acquires property rights and the owner loses them. Eminent domain is a government's power to confiscate private property for public use. The U.S. Constitution requires just compensation for property taken by eminent domain.

15. The different approaches to taxing a corporation's earnings in the context of international commerce are the following:
    - Territorial tax systems
    - Worldwide tax system
    - Border tax adjustments
    - Earnings stripping
    - Inversion

16. A business should consider the following when establishing a subsidiary in an offshore tax haven:
    - The country's tax structure
    - The country's level of enforcement of its privacy laws
    - The country's language
    - The type of judicial system the country has
    - The country's political stability
    - The country's independence from the parent company's home country
    - The costs of establishing the new subsidiary in the country

17. Repatriation of earnings is the process by which a U.S. parent company moves earnings from its foreign-based affiliates back to the U.S. to the parent company or its stockholders.

18. Five U.S. laws changed by the Patriot Act are the following (any five):
    - Wiretap Statute (Title III)
    - Electronic Communications Privacy Act
    - Computer Fraud and Abuse Act
    - Foreign Intelligence Surveillance Act (FISA)
    - Family Education Rights and Privacy Act
    - Pen Register and Trap and Trace Statutes
    - Money Laundering Act
    - Immigration and Nationality Act

- Money Laundering Control Act
- Bank Secrecy Act
- Right to Financial Privacy Act
- Fair Credit Reporting Act

19. The United Nations' purposes are the following:
    - To maintain international peace and security
    - To develop friendly relations among nations
    - To cooperate in solving international economic, social, cultural, and humanitarian problems
    - To promote respect for human rights and fundamental freedoms
    - To be a center for harmonizing the actions of nations in attaining these goals

20. The following are three primary WTO agreements:
    (1) The General Agreement on Tariffs and Trade (GATT)
    (2) The General Agreement on Trade in Services (GATS)
    (3) The Agreement on Trade-Related Aspects of Intellectual Property Rights (TRIPS Agreement)

21. NAFTA applies to Canada, Mexico, and the U.S.

22. NAFTA eliminated nearly all tariffs between the U.S. and Canada by 1998 and is to eliminate nearly all tariffs between the U.S. and Mexico by 2008.

23. ASEAN is the Association of Southeast Asian Nations, which includes the member states of Indonesia, Malaysia, Philippines, Singapore, Thailand, Brunei Darussalam, Vietnam, Laos, Myanmar, and Cambodia. Its purposes are to accelerate the economic growth, social progress, and cultural development of the region and to promote regional peace and stability through respect for justice and the rule of law.

24. APEC is the Asia-Pacific Economic Cooperation. It attempts to facilitate economic growth, cooperation, trade, and investment in the Asia-Pacific region and is the only inter-governmental body that operates on the basis of nonbinding commitments, open dialogue, and equal respect for the views of all participant countries.

Application Questions

1. a. FIC would own or control any subsidiaries, which would issue stock. FIC could own 100 percent of the stock, giving it the highest level of control, or it could trade shares publicly in foreign markets. Some foreign markets might require FIC to form subsidiaries to bring their operations under local laws or incorporation. This option would provide a higher level of a risk with higher returns. Use of subsidiaries is best for a company experienced in international operations, so FIC's lack of experience could be a disadvantage for this option. The time required for implementing this option could vary by country, and development of subsidiaries from the ground up could take years, with large investments of resources and time.

   b. FIC's forming joint ventures would involve shared ownership and control, offering high earnings and growth potential and more options for entry into foreign markets. This option commonly would involve joining forces with a second company in each country. One disadvantage is that, because of its specialized business, FIC might not find suitable insurers (or any insurers at all) with which to form joint ventures in some countries, particularly those that have no similar insurers in existence. Although, like subsidiaries, joint ventures increase companies' business risk and commitment of resources, with substantial capital, the value of a joint venture can be greater than the sum of what the individual partners contribute. Choosing the right partners could be the most problematic issue.

2. In Peru, FIC could face the following challenges: Language, culture, and distance, and space. Time differences probably would not be a problem because Peru is in a similar time zone.

    In Liberia, FIC could face the following challenges: Distance and space, culture, and time. The company should research what language problems might arise as well as the stability of the government.

3. The company should research how the countries tax foreign income and how businesses are taxed for income made from internal business as well as external business.

Exam Information

About Institute Exams

Exam questions are based on the Educational Objectives stated in the course guide and textbook. The exam is designed to measure whether you have met those Educational Objectives. The exam does not test every Educational Objective. Instead, it tests over a balanced sample of Educational Objectives.

How to Prepare for Institute Exams

What can you do to prepare for an Institute exam? Students who pass Institute exams do the following:

▶ Use the assigned study materials. Focus your study on the Educational Objectives presented at the beginning of each course guide assignment. Thoroughly read the textbook and any other assigned materials, and then complete the course guide exercises. Choose a study method that best suits your needs; for example, participate in a traditional class, online class, or informal study group; or study on your own. Use the Institutes' SMART Study Aids (if available) for practice and review. If this course has an associated SMART Online Practice Exams product, you will find an access code on the inside back cover of this course guide. This access code allows you to print (in PDF format) a full practice exam and to take additional online practice exams that will simulate an actual credentialing exam.

▶ Become familiar with the types of test questions asked on the exam. The practice exam in this course guide or in the SMART Online Practice Exams product will help you understand the different types of questions you will encounter on the exam.

▶ Maximize your test-taking time. Successful students use the sample exam in the course guide or in the SMART Online Practice Exams product to practice pacing themselves. Learning how to manage your time during the exam ensures that you will complete all of the test questions in the time allotted.

Types of Exam Questions

The exam for this course consists of objective questions of several types.

The Correct-Answer Type

In this type of question, the question stem is followed by four responses, one of which is absolutely correct. Select the *correct* answer.

> Which one of the following persons evaluates requests for insurance to determine which applicants are accepted and which are rejected?
>
> a.   The premium auditor
>
> b.   The loss control representative
>
> c.   The underwriter
>
> d.   The risk manager

The Best-Answer Type

In this type of question, the question stem is followed by four responses, only one of which is best, given the statement made or facts provided in the stem. Select the *best* answer.

> Several people within an insurer might be involved in determining whether an applicant for insurance is accepted. Which one of the following positions is primarily responsible for determining whether an applicant for insurance is accepted?
>
> a.   The loss control representative
>
> b.   The customer service representative
>
> c.   The underwriter
>
> d.   The premium auditor

The Incomplete-Statement or Sentence-Completion Type

In this type of question, the last part of the question stem consists of a portion of a statement rather than a direct question. Select the phrase that *correctly* or *best* completes the sentence.

> Residual market plans designed for individuals who are unable to obtain insurance on their personal property in the voluntary market are called
>
> a. VIN plans.
>
> b. Self-insured retention plans.
>
> c. Premium discount plans.
>
> d. FAIR plans.

"All of the Above" Type

In this type of question, only one of the first three answers could be correct, or all three might be correct, in which case the best answer would be "All of the above." Read all the answers and select the *best* answer.

> When a large commercial insured's policy is up for renewal, who is likely to provide input to the renewal decision process?
>
> a. The underwriter
>
> b. The loss control representative
>
> c. The producer
>
> d. All of the above

"All of the following, EXCEPT:" Type

In this type of question, responses include three correct answers and one answer that is incorrect or is clearly the least correct. Select the *incorrect* or *least correct* answer.

> All of the following adjust insurance claims, EXCEPT:
>
> a. Insurer claim representatives
>
> b. Premium auditors
>
> c. Producers
>
> d. Independent adjusters

About the Code of Professional Ethics

This is a brief summary of information appearing in greater detail in the Code of Professional Ethics, which is among the CPCU 510 study materials.

All CPCU candidates and CPCUs are bound by the Code of Professional Ethics of the American Institute for CPCU. The Code describes both high goals and minimum standards of conduct.

1. The high goals described in the Canons challenge all CPCUs and CPCU candidates to aspire to the highest level of ethical performance in all of their professional activities.

2. The minimum standards of conduct, described in the Rules, maintain the integrity of the CPCU designation. CPCUs and CPCU candidates are obligated to at least meet the minimum standards in the Rules, and failure to do so may subject a CPCU—or a CPCU candidate—to disciplinary measures.

CPCU candidates study the Code and are tested in CPCU 510 to ensure that all CPCUs understand their ethical obligations. The ultimate goal of the Code is to foster highly ethical conduct on the part of all CPCUs.

The Canons and Rules of the Code of Professional Ethics

Canon 1—CPCUs should endeavor at all times to place the public interest above their own.

Rule R1.1—A CPCU has a duty to understand and abide by all *Rules* of conduct which are prescribed in the *Code of Professional Ethics of the American Institute*.

Rule R1.2—A CPCU shall not advocate, sanction, participate in, cause to be accomplished, otherwise carry out through another, or condone any act which the CPCU is prohibited from performing by the *Rules* of this *Code*.

Canon 2—CPCUs should seek continually to maintain and improve their professional knowledge, skills, and competence.

Rule R2.1—A CPCU shall keep informed on those technical matters that are essential to the maintenance of the CPCU's professional competence in insurance, risk management, or related fields.

Canon 3—CPCUs should obey all laws and regulations, and should avoid any conduct or activity which would cause unjust harm to others.

Rule R3.1—In the conduct of business or professional activities, a CPCU shall not engage in any act or omission of a dishonest, deceitful, or fraudulent nature.

Rule R3.2—A CPCU shall not allow the pursuit of financial gain or other personal benefit to interfere with the exercise of sound professional judgment and skills.

Rule R3.3—A CPCU shall not violate any law or regulation relating to professional activities or commit any felony.

Canon 4—CPCUs should be diligent in the performance of their occupational duties and should continually strive to improve the functioning of the insurance mechanism.

Rule R4.1—A CPCU shall competently and consistently discharge his or her occupational duties.

Rule R4.2—A CPCU shall support efforts to effect such improvements in claims settlement, contract design, investment, marketing, pricing, reinsurance, safety engineering, underwriting, and other insurance operations as will both inure to the benefit of the public and improve the overall efficiency with which the insurance mechanism functions.

Canon 5—CPCUs should assist in maintaining and raising professional standards in the insurance business.

Rule R5.1—A CPCU shall support personnel policies and practices which will attract qualified individuals to the insurance business, provide them with ample and equal opportunities for advancement, and encourage them to aspire to the highest levels of professional competence and achievement.

Rule R5.2—A CPCU shall encourage and assist qualified individuals who wish to pursue CPCU or other studies which will enhance their professional competence.

Rule R5.3—A CPCU shall support the development, improvement, and enforcement of such laws, regulations, and codes as will foster competence and ethical conduct on the part of all insurance practitioners and inure to the benefit of the public.

Rule R5.4—A CPCU shall not withhold information or assistance officially requested by appropriate regulatory authorities who are investigating or prosecuting any alleged violation of the laws or regulations governing the qualifications or conduct of insurance practitioners.

Canon 6—CPCUs should strive to establish and maintain dignified and honorable relationships with those whom they serve, with fellow insurance practitioners, and with members of other professions.

Rule R6.1—A CPCU shall keep informed on the legal limitations imposed upon the scope of his or her professional activities.

Rule R6.2—A CPCU shall not disclose to another person any confidential information entrusted to, or obtained by, the CPCU in the course of the CPCU's business or professional activities, unless a disclosure of such information is required by law or is made to a person who necessarily must have the information in order to discharge legitimate occupational or professional duties.

Rule R6.3—In rendering or proposing to render professional services for others, a CPCU shall not knowingly misrepresent or conceal any limitations on the CPCU's ability to provide the quantity or quality of professional services required by the circumstances.

Canon 7—CPCUs should assist in improving the public understanding of insurance and risk management.

Rule R7.1—A CPCU shall support efforts to provide members of the public with objective information concerning their risk management and insurance needs and the products, services, and techniques which are available to meet their needs.

Rule R7.2—A CPCU shall not misrepresent the benefits, costs, or limitations of any risk management technique or any product or service of an insurer.

Canon 8—CPCUs should honor the integrity of the CPCU designation and respect the limitations placed on its use.

Rule R8.1—A CPCU shall use the CPCU designation and the CPCU key only in accordance with the relevant *Guidelines* promulgated by the American Institute.

Rule R8.2—A CPCU shall not attribute to the mere possession of the designation depth or scope of knowledge, skills, and professional capabilities greater than those demonstrated by successful completion of the CPCU program.

Rule R8.3—A CPCU shall not make unfair comparisons between a person who holds the CPCU designation and one who does not.

Rule R8.4—A CPCU shall not write, speak, or act in such a way as to lead another to reasonably believe the CPCU is officially representing the American Institute, unless the CPCU has been duly authorized to do so by the American Institute.

Canon 9—CPCUs should assist in maintaining the integrity of the *Code of Professional Ethics*.

Rule R9.1—A CPCU shall not initiate or support the CPCU candidacy of any individual known by the CPCU to engage in business practices which violate the ethical standards prescribed by this *Code*.

Rule R9.2—A CPCU possessing unprivileged information concerning an alleged violation of this *Code* shall, upon request, reveal such information to the tribunal or other authority empowered by the American Institute to investigate or act upon the alleged violation.

Rule R9.3—A CPCU shall report promptly to the American Institute any information concerning the use of the CPCU designation by an unauthorized person.